Some Social Practice

---

compiled and written by **Ellen Mueller**

CONTENTS

INTRODUCTION

This book is a compilation of short-run one-page folded informational zines on the topic of social practice. For those unfamiliar with the medium, zines are small-circulation self-published (traditionally printed) works containing text and/ or images on a particular topic.

I started making these inexpensive colorful zines while I was working at a university where I was tasked with writing new social practice curriculum for a curious student body, who were largely unfamiliar with social practice. The first zines examined definitions and spectrums. As I visited classes and spoke about social practice, I handed out a few of these zines to help frame our conversations about this often nebulous field of study. Students appreciated having some easily accessible foundational information to consider as they dove into these new (to them) ideas and practices.

Then, I created additional zines to address the recurring questions I received about social practice -- usually as people tried to better understand the field's boundaries and history. Through this process, I realized the collection of zines could also serve as the framework for a course others might like to build on. To that end, this book contains the original 20 zines, as well as expanded information in areas where I was unable to include as much content as I would have liked due to the space restrictions of the single-sheet format. Further, all the social practice examples are now sorted into a single timeline for easy chronological navigation. There are also sample syllabi and assignments, which build on the content of this book.

My hope is that this book will act as a basic introduction to the field of social practice, whether as a textbook, or as a course planning resource. To assist in further researching specific areas, readers will notice citations and lists of books and online resources throughout the text. This approach supports my aim to keep the text as practical, useful, and succinct as possible in every way.

Lastly, acknowledging the long-standing role of publication in social practice, and as a proponent of Creative Commons licensing, which provides several options for making creative works available for others to build upon legally and to share, self-publishing this book felt like a natural next step in the distribution of the zines. This book is licensed under the *Creative Commons Attribution-NonCommercial-ShareAlike License*. This license lets others remix, tweak, and build upon this work non-commercially, as long as they credit the author (myself, Ellen Mueller) and license their new creations under identical terms.

Engagement, Socially Engaged Practices / Art, Community
Development, Interactive/Participatory, Relational Practices,
Civic Practice / Art, Contextual Practice, Artistic Activism,
Creative Placemaking, Social Practice, Community
Arts/Practice, Dialogical Practices, Community Engagement,
Public Practice, Public Forms, Performative Engagement

Definitions of Social Practice

Interactive / Participatory, Relational Practices, Civic Practice
/ Art, Contextual Practice, Artistic Activism, Creative
Placemaking, Cultural Organizing, Participatory Art, Social
Sculpture, Civic Practice, Social Practice, Community Arts /
Practice, Dialogical Practices, Community Engagement,
Public Practice, Public Forms, Performative Engagement,
Socially Engaged Practices / Art, Community Development,
Interactive/Participatory, Relational Practices, Civic Practice /
Art, Contextual Practice, Artistic Activism, Creative
Placemaking, Social Practice, Community Arts / Practice,
Dialogical Practices, Community Engagement, Public
Practice, Public Forms, Performative Engagement, Socially
Engaged Practices / Art, Community Development,
Interactive / Participatory, Relational Practices Civic Practice
/ Art, Contextual Practice, Artistic Activism Creative
Placemaking, Cultural Organizing, Participatory Art, Social
Sculpture, Civic Practice, Social Practice, Community Arts /
Practice, Dialogical Practices, Community Engagement,
Public Practice, Public Forms, Performative Engagement
, Socially Engaged Practices / Art, Community Development,

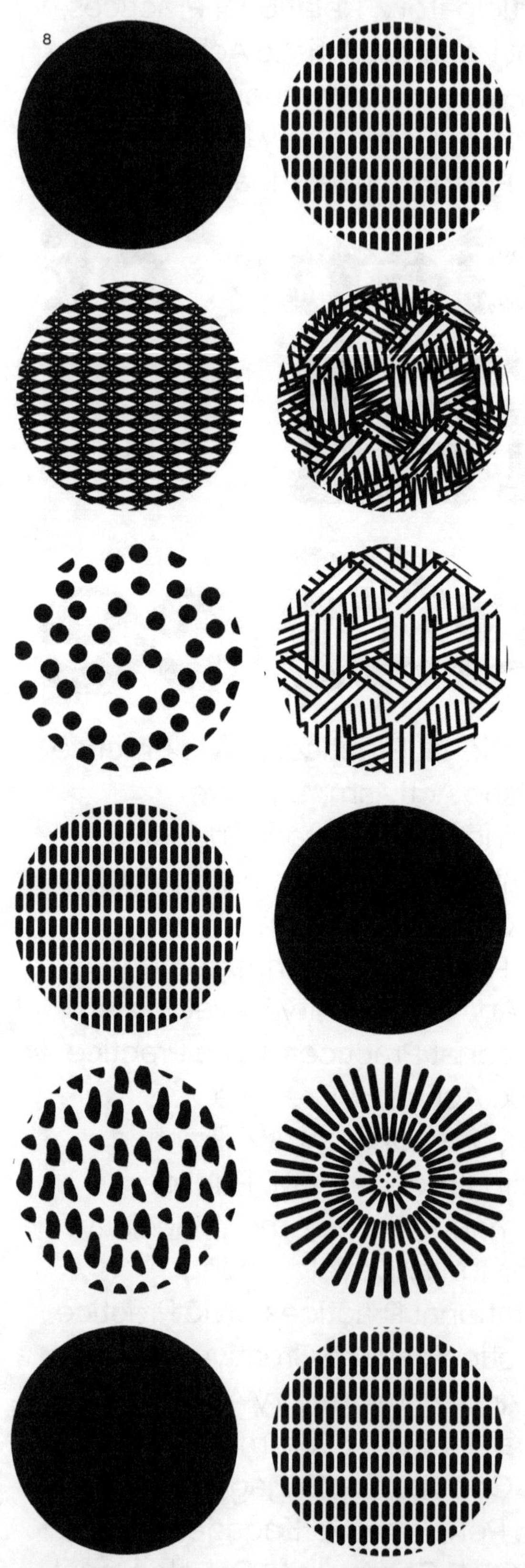

"Socially engaged art is a hybrid, multi-disciplinary activity that exists somewhere between art and non-art, and its state may be permanently unresolved. Socially engaged art depends on actual — not imagined or hypothetical — social action."

–Pablo Helguera
Education for Socially Engaged Art

It is "the opposite of studio practice. It's not all about the artist, and it isn't assumed that work will go into a gallery." It doesn't have a look, like Cubism or Pop Art, and it has no central message, like Expressionism or Surrealism.

–Harell Fletcher
https://goo.gl/zUVUcM

There is also the argument that socially engaged art may not always address political or economic issues — certain expressions of cultural identity are political acts unto themselves.

–http://artmakingchange.org

Social practice is "a term that combines aesthetics and politics, as a term for art events that are inter-relational, embodied, and durational… celebrat[ing] a degree of cross-disciplinarity… gestur[ing] to the realm of the socio-political" and "resolutely imprecise."

–Shannon Jackson
Social Works: Performing Art, Supporting Publics

Artistic practice that works with and for the benefit of communities. Helicon Collaborative offered this working definition: "artistic or creative practice that aims to improve conditions in a particular community or in the world at large." They found this kind of art assumes artists have agency and responsibility to affect social change, and often entails collaborating closely with community members. As such it requires forms and materials that go beyond those used in studio art.

–http://artmakingchange.org

"…people constitute the central artistic medium and material…"

–Claire Bishop
Artificial Hells

Social practice, "... does not hang well in a museum, and it isn't commercially viable..."; it, "... includes careful listening, thoughtful conversation, and community organizing... social practice artists create forms of living that activate communities and advance public awareness of pressing social issues."

–Nato Thompson
Living as Form

"Grandma, social practice is when someone devotes an extraordinary amount of time, energy, and attention to relationships between people."

–Bryce Dwyer
"How do you explain social practice to your grandmother?" in *The Questions We Ask Together*

"Social practice reveals our mutual dependencies upon one another, yet the generosity, acceptance and reciprocity that such work demands is difficult to establish and even more challenging to sustain"

–Amy M. Mooney and Neysa Page-Lieberman
The Quandary of Social Practice: Why Empathy? Why Risk?

"... artworks that not only openly question the larger sociopolitical and cultural context of which they are a part, but also strive to produce or strengthen the very foundations upon which collective inquiry can function."

–Lisa Phillips
"Director's Forward" in *Public Servants: Art and the Crisis of the Common Good*

It amplifies the creativity that already exists within communities by using arts and culture to build community networks, solve problems, and enhance our sense of ownership in the places where we live, work, and grow. Helping everyday people know the power of their own creative capacity to transform their lives, their relationships, and their surroundings.

–*http://laundromatproject.org*

It "is about artists collaborating with people in communities." The aim is to bring about heightened awareness of societal, cultural, ecological or political issues that are of immediate concern to that community.

–*Mark Tribe*
https://goo.gl/zUVUcM

Both SEA [Socially Engaged Art] and SEC [Socially Engaged Craft] take "social engagement" as both their subject and material.

–*Mary Callahan Baumstark*
"Traversing Topographies: Craftivism and Socially Engaged Craft in Conversation" in *Social Objects*

"[I]ts practitioners freely blur the lines among object making, performance, political activism, community organizing, environmentalism and investigative journalism, creating a deeply participatory art that often flourishes outside the gallery and museum system."

–*Randy Kennedy*
"Outside the Citadel, Social Practice Art Is Intended to Nurture," in *New York Times*

"True community is more than a technique or a practice, but a praxis to transcend individual privileges, where separate expectations are replaced with equality and collective interest. By creating experience of dynamic demographics, with exercises that everyone can create in, there is a unification of new community that is inclusive in its being."

–Brett Cook
"Isn't all art "Social Practice"?"
in *The Questions We Ask Together*

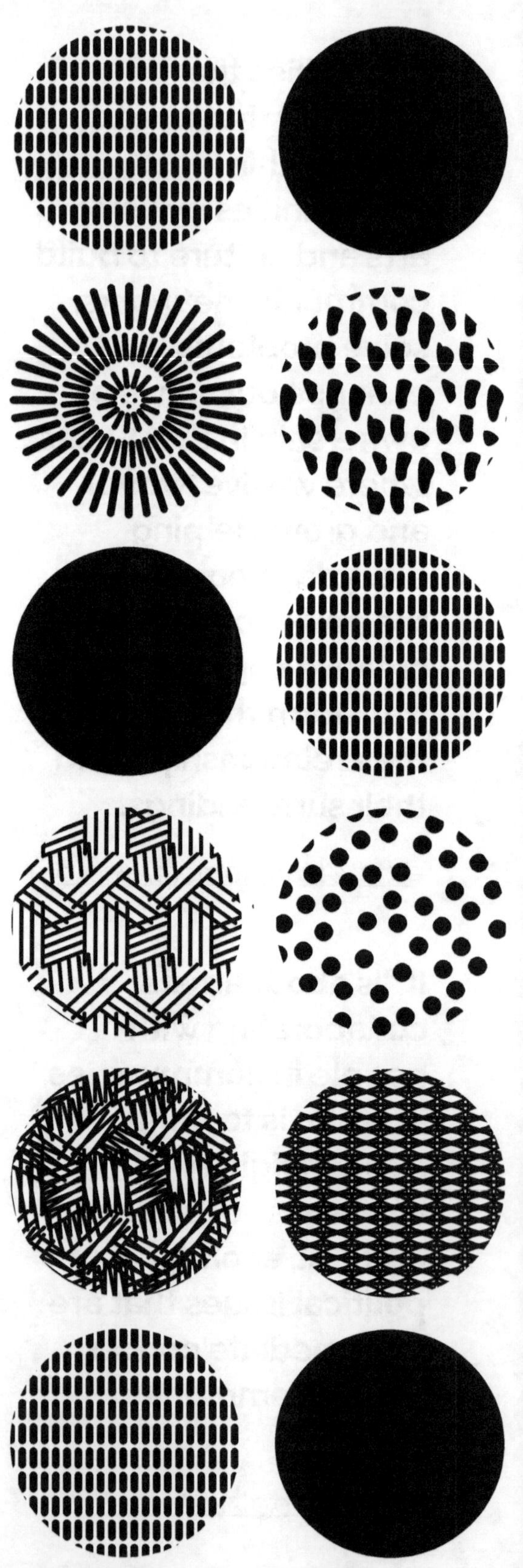

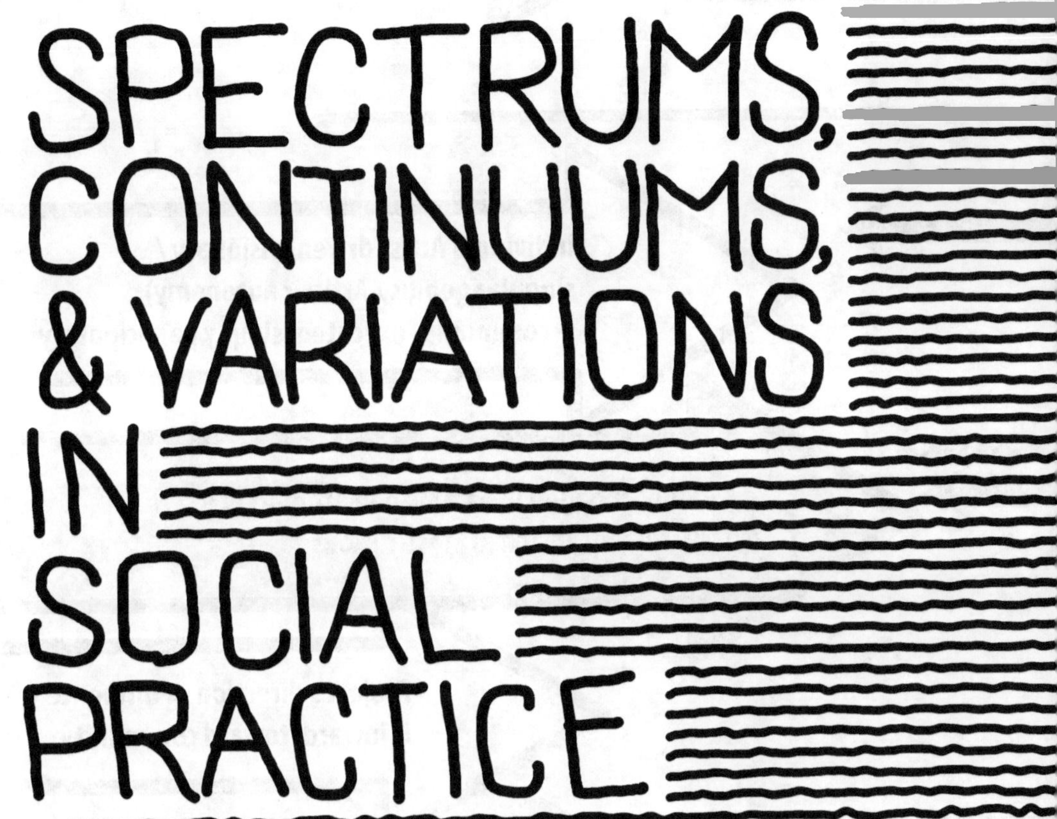

SPECTRUMS, CONTINUUMS, & VARIATIONS IN SOCIAL PRACTICE

The artist is from outside the community

Individual Artist driven (visionary /
singular genius / Artistic autonomy)
+ community executed; simply participatory

Fully engaged in established art market;
Occurring within art institutions

Project's direction of influence
is inward, toward community

The project originated outside the community

includes poetic (small gestures); fine art
aesthetics; express or represent an idea

Object-based (product-based)   Full ephemeral (process-based)

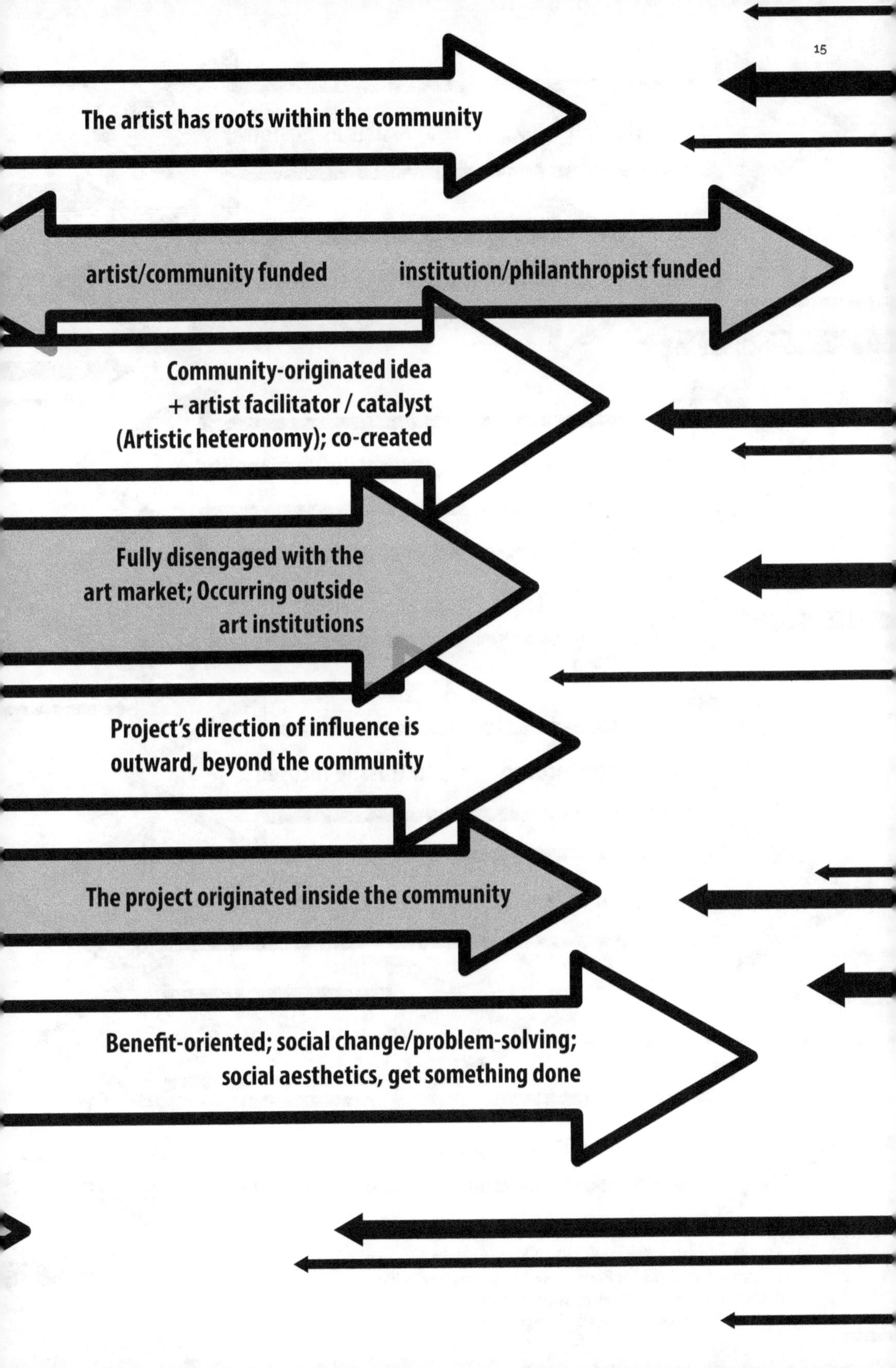

The artist has roots within the community

artist/community funded   institution/philanthropist funded

Community-originated idea
+ artist facilitator / catalyst
(Artistic heteronomy); co-created

Fully disengaged with the
art market; Occurring outside
art institutions

Project's direction of influence is
outward, beyond the community

The project originated inside the community

Benefit-oriented; social change/problem-solving;
social aesthetics, get something done

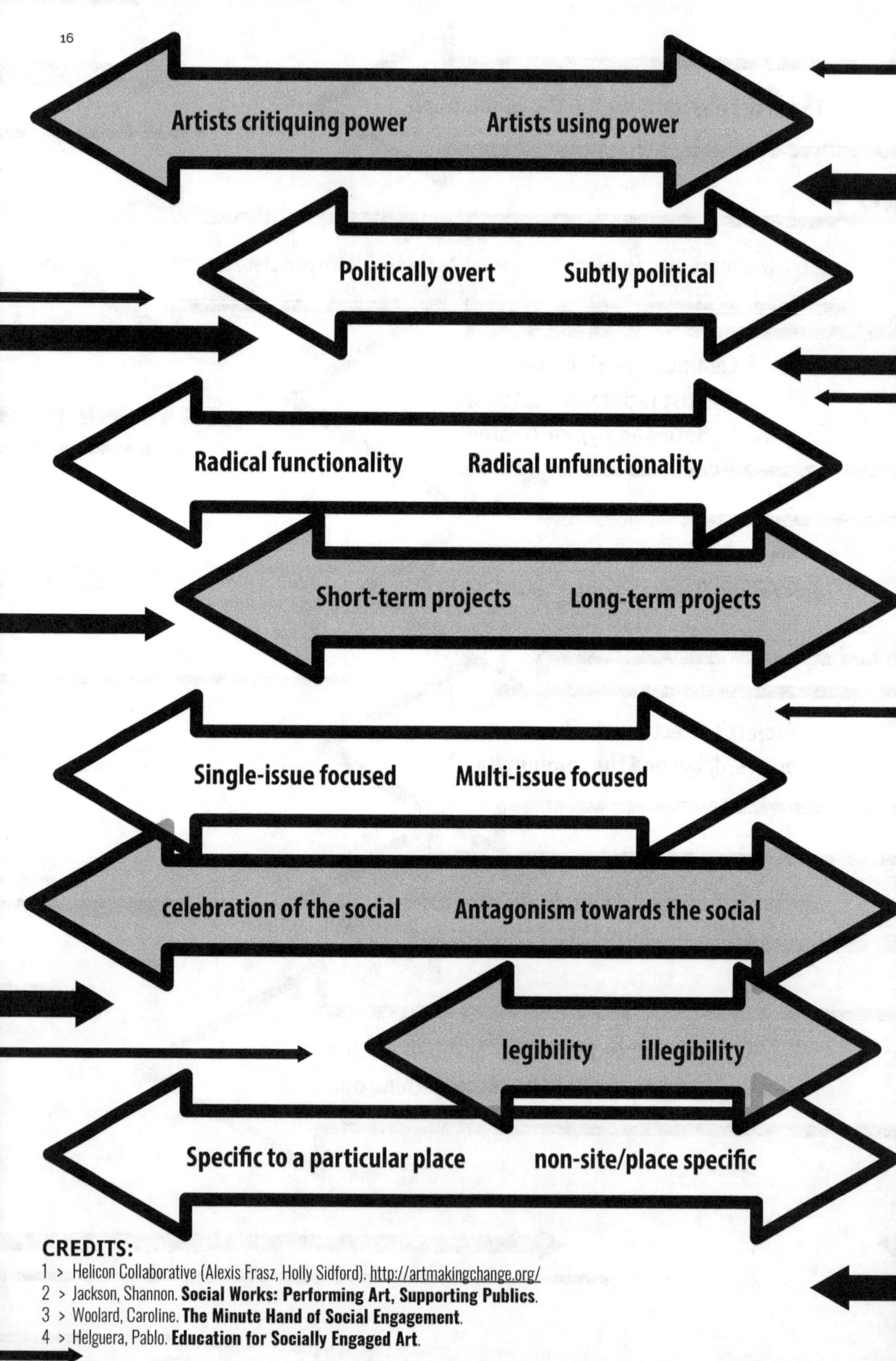

CREDITS:

1 > Helicon Collaborative (Alexis Frasz, Holly Sidford). http://artmakingchange.org/
2 > Jackson, Shannon. **Social Works: Performing Art, Supporting Publics**.
3 > Woolard, Caroline. **The Minute Hand of Social Engagement**.
4 > Helguera, Pablo. **Education for Socially Engaged Art**.

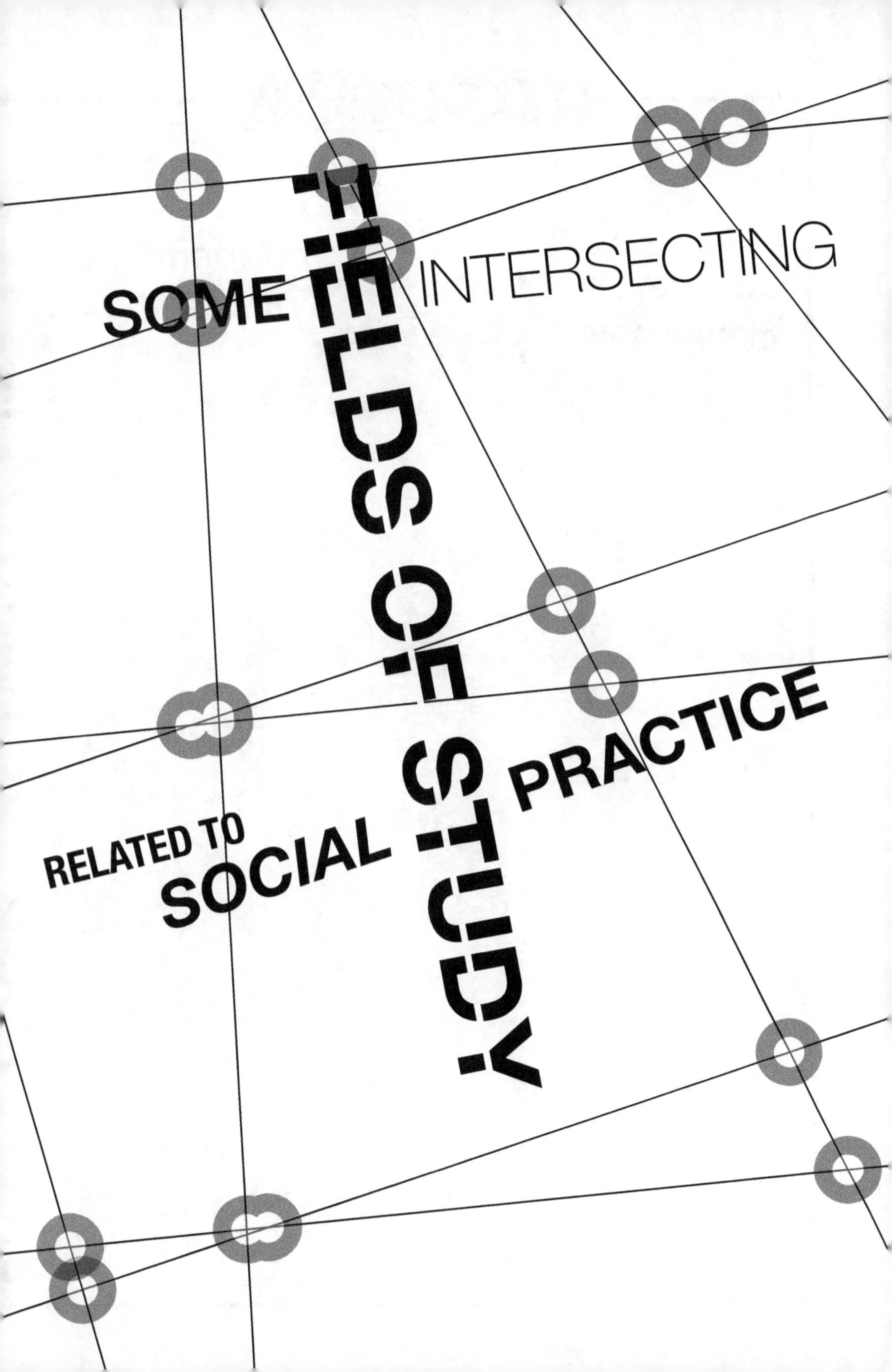

SOME INTERSECTING
FIELDS OF STUDY
RELATED TO SOCIAL PRACTICE

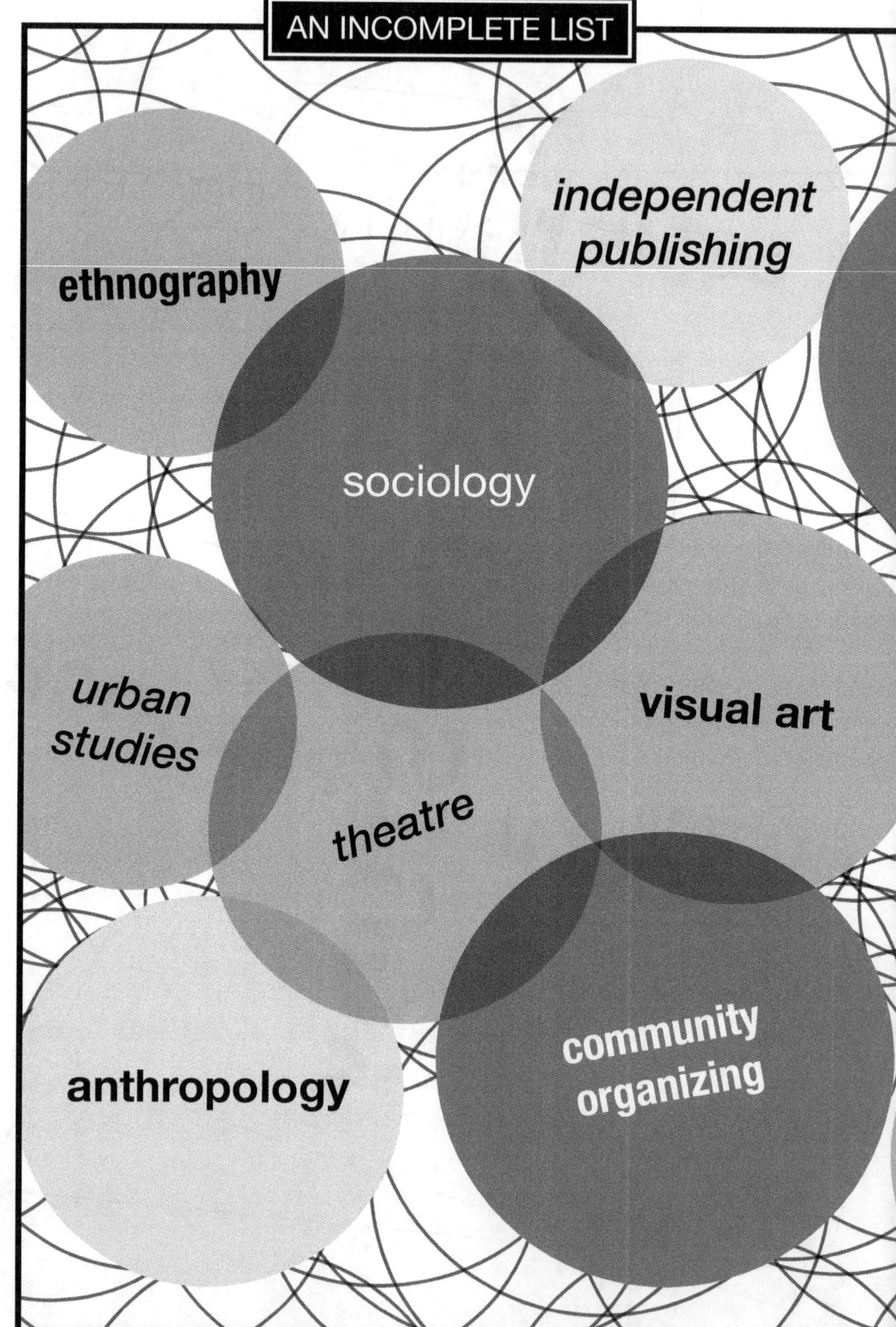
AN INCOMPLETE LIST
ethnography
independent publishing
sociology
urban studies
visual art
theatre
anthropology
community organizing

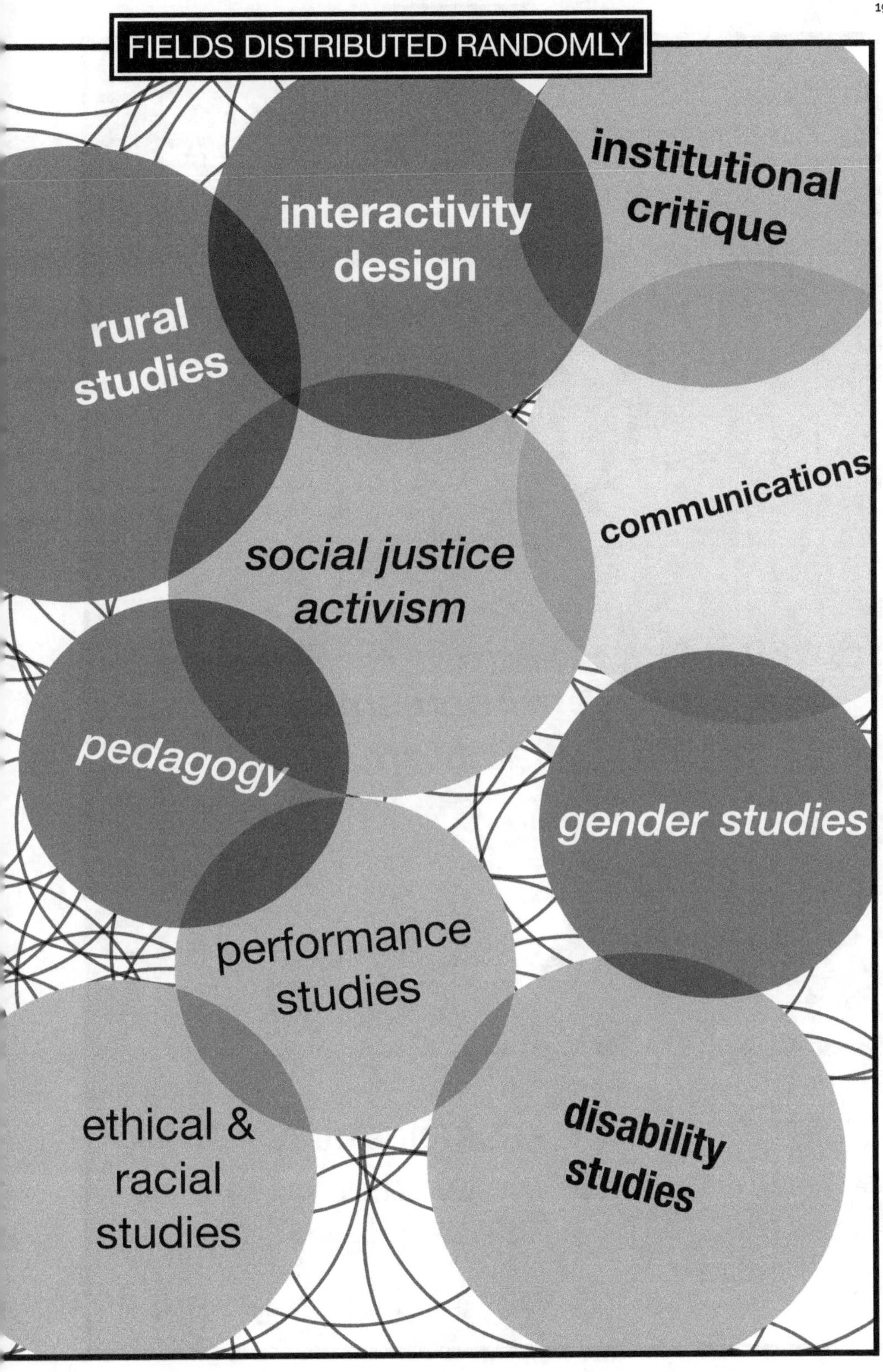

FIELDS DISTRIBUTED RANDOMLY
interactivity design
institutional critique
rural studies
communications
social justice activism
pedagogy
gender studies
performance studies
ethical & racial studies
disability studies

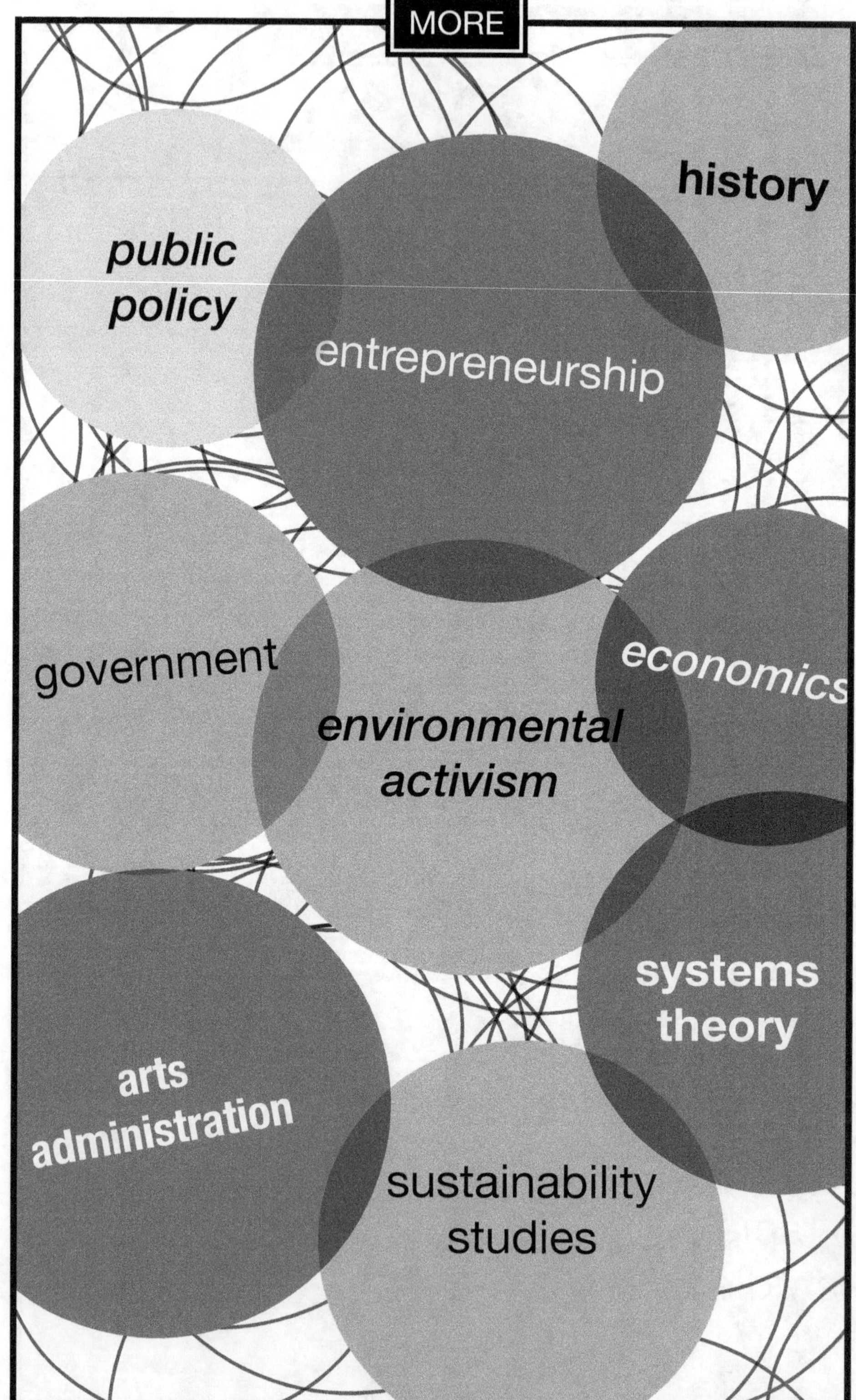

MORE
history
public policy
entrepreneurship
government
economics
environmental activism
systems theory
arts administration
sustainability studies

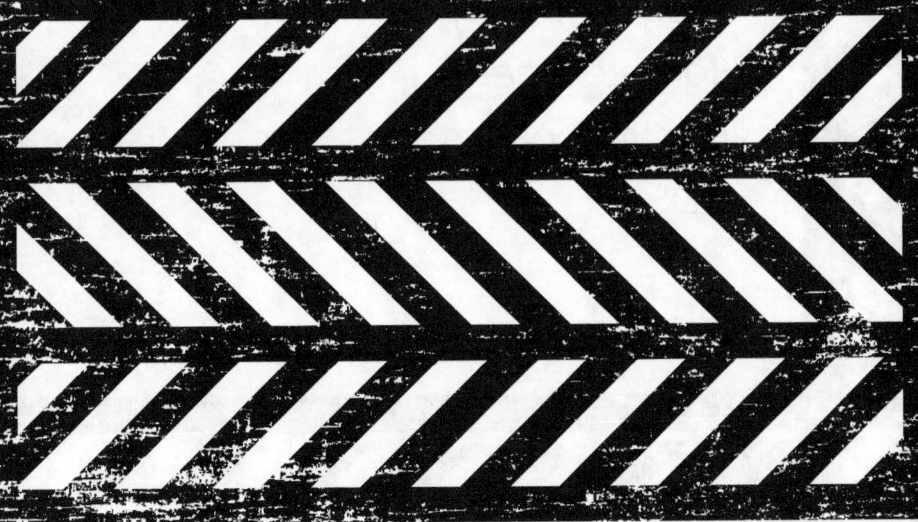
SOME SYSTEMS/TOPICS
SOCIAL PRACTICE
FREQUENTLY
TOUCHES ON

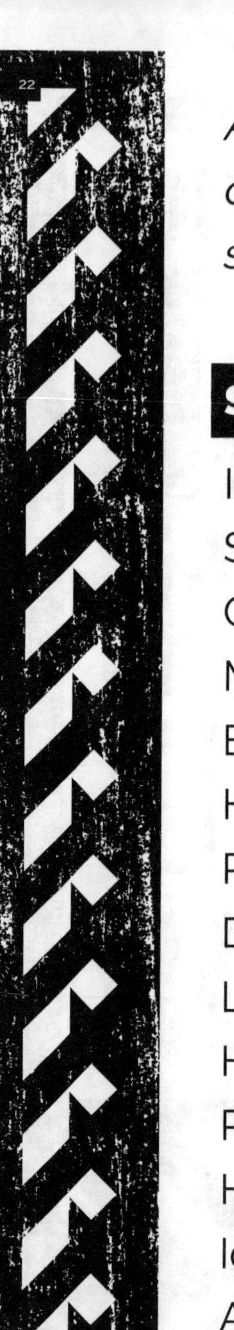

All of these areas have a great deal of overlap, and this is just a sampling of systems/topics.

SOCIAL JUSTICE

Indigenous rights

Structural racism

Gender issues/women's rights

Migration/citizenship/immigration

Equity

Health care

Poverty

Disability issues

LGBTQ issues

Human rights

Police brutality

Homelessness

Identity politics

AIDS

ENVIRONMENT

Land use

Climate change

Sustainability

Health

Energy

Parks and open spaces

Habitat restoration

CAPITALISM/BUSINESS/INDUSTRY

Affordable housing

Food policy/scarcity

Labor issues

Technology

Supply chains

Art funding

Consumerism

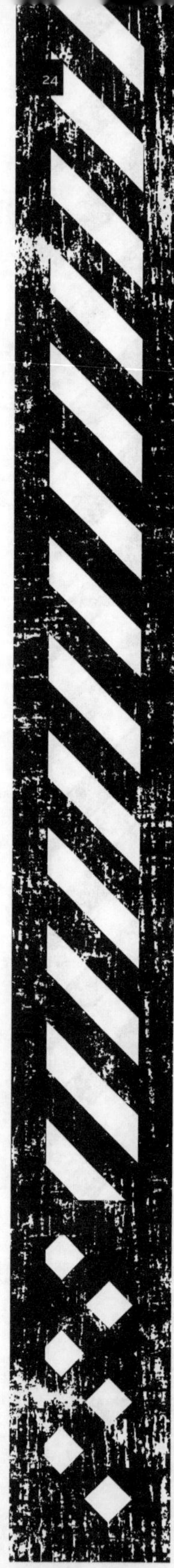

EDUCATION

Ethics

Access

DEMOCRACY/GOVERNMENT

Infrastructure

Policy development

Public safety

Power Relationships

Media Access

Revolution

War

Representation

LOCALNESS/PLACE

Rural vs Urban

Transportation

Art/Life boundary

Gentrification

Community building

History & memory

CREDITS:
1 > http://welcometocup.org
2 > http://creativetime.org/programs/archive/2011/livingasform/archive.htm

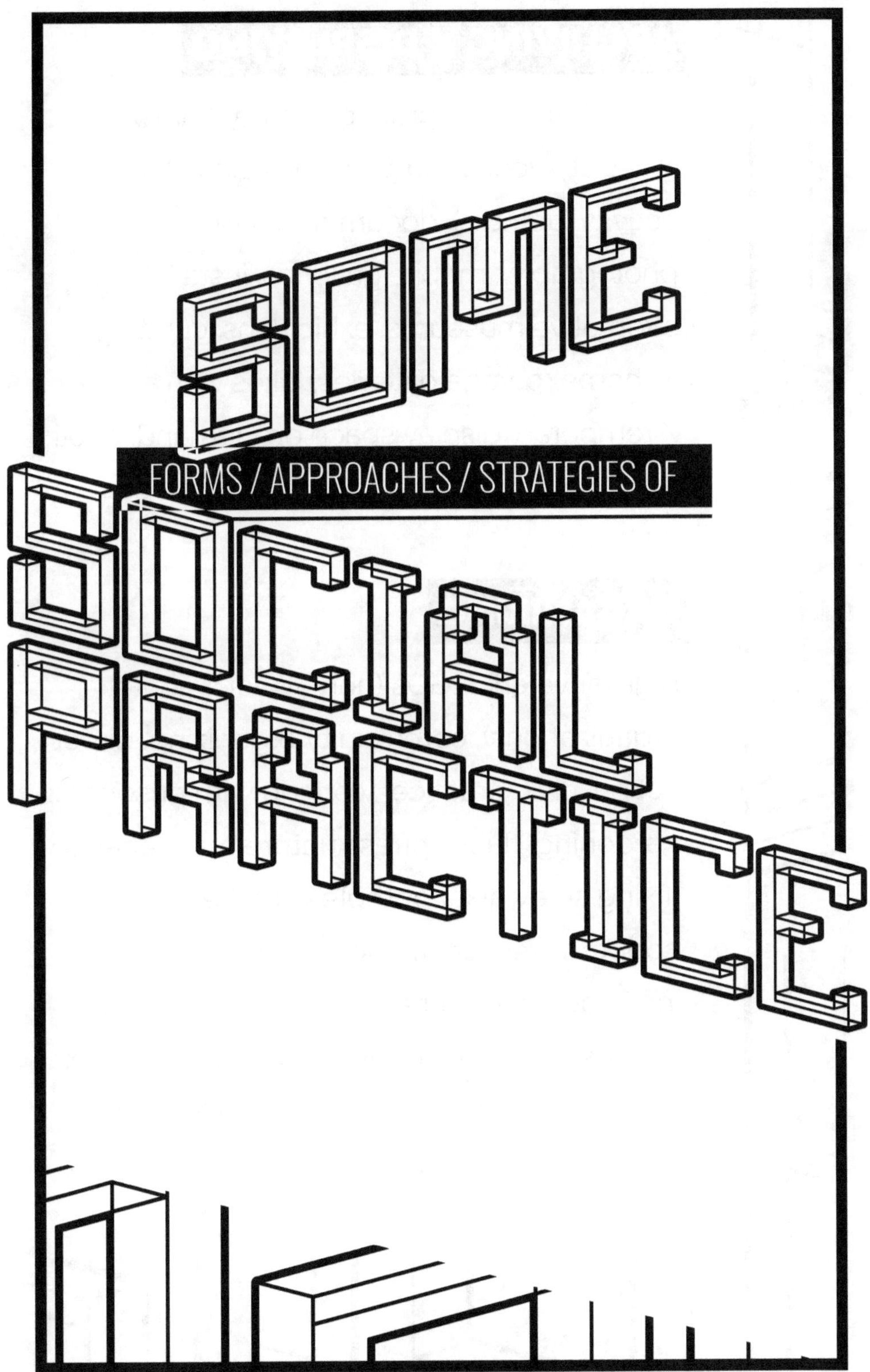

SOME
FORMS / APPROACHES / STRATEGIES OF
SOCIAL PRACTICE

ARCHIVING / DISPLAYING

tablecloths for capturing written / drawn ideas at events, sculptural remains of an activity (detritus), documentary video, photography, mobile galleries, installations, alternative museums, exhibitions, curating, in-home/garage galleries, bikes with a trailer / temporary display space on-demand, public art, monuments, web-based projects, etc.

ORGANIZING

legislative art, NGOs (non-governmental organizations), community organizing, direct action, civic practice, working with prisoners, gardening, flags, infrastructure maintenance (fixing sidewalks/potholes), real estate cooperatives, providing missing services to incite action (internet connectivity, library spaces, etc.), faux or alternative government bodies for envisioning change/difference, wellness clinics, etc.

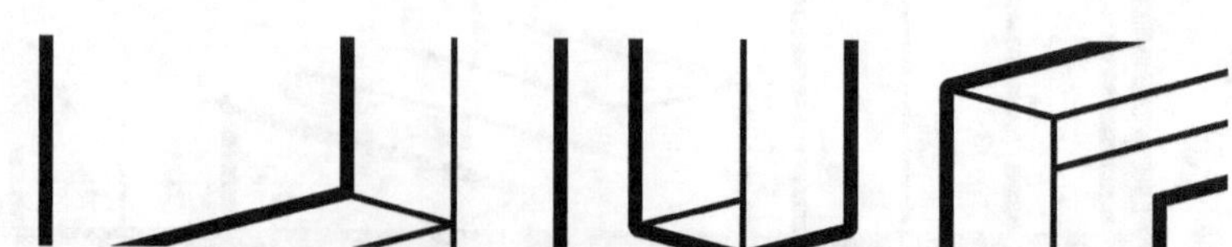

EDUCATING

temporary classrooms, alternative schools, interactive media, alternative pedagogy, creating/distributing literature, workshops, conferences, some artist residencies, tours (live versus audio), zines/informational publications, artist books, map making, slide shows, campaigns, advocacy, etc.

GATHERING/TALKING

facilitated exchanges, online networks, manifesto writing/sharing, large public chalkboards, a pop-up radio station, group sketching, sharing a megaphone, protests, etc.

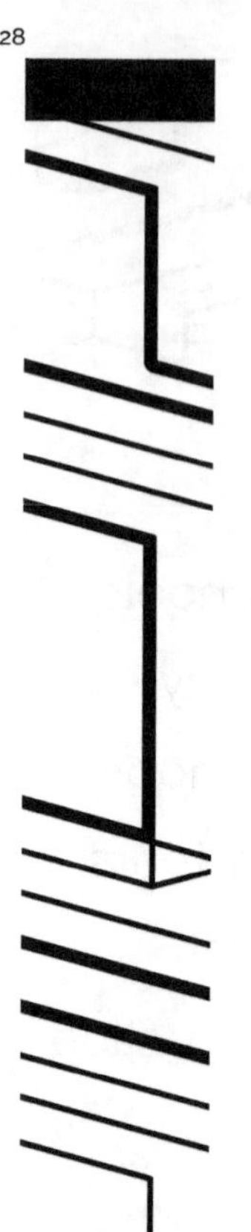

EVENTS

parties, feasts/potlucks/community cookouts, fashion shows, athletic events, reenactments, parades, press briefings, performances, karaoke, gift-giving, etc.

INFRASTRUCTURE

hub spaces [part workshop venue, part office, part exhibition space, part interpretive center, part event amplifier], playgrounds/gymnasiums, recycling/reusing/borrowing centers (tool check-out, co-op maker spaces, bike maintenance spaces with tools), restaurants, mobile infrastructure for interactions that can be deployed across a city, invented new objects, alternative currencies, etc.

CREDITS:
1 > Amy M. Mooney and Neysa Page-Lieberman, **The Quandary of Social Practice: Why Empathy? Why Risk?**
2 > http://artmakingchange.org/
3 > http://creativetime.org/programs/archive/2011/livingasform/archive.htm

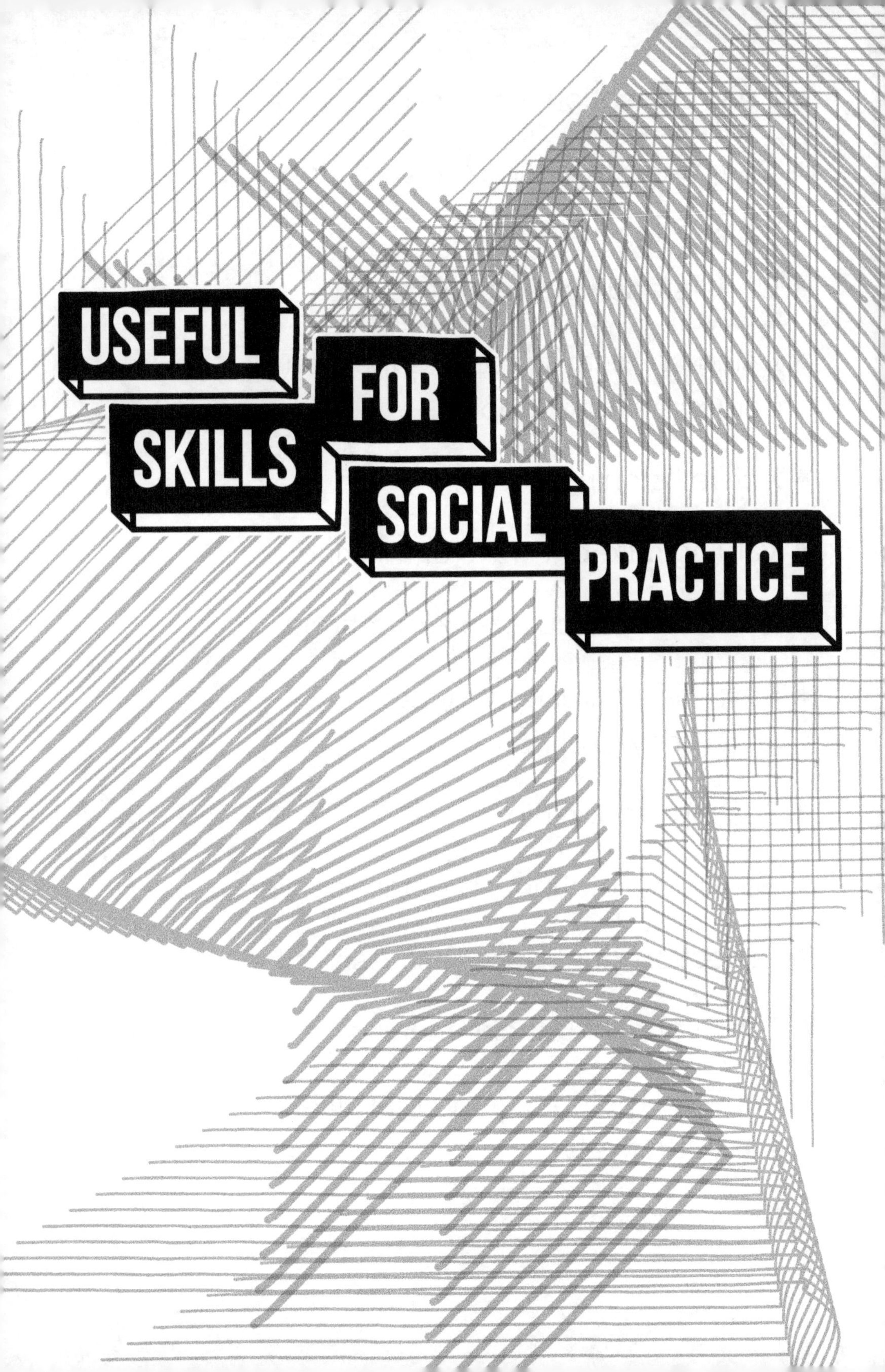

USEFUL
SKILLS
FOR
SOCIAL
PRACTICE

* Communication (written, oral, visual)

* Community building/organization/ leadership

* Understanding of ethics

* Using physical space to support a democratic philosophy

* Active listening

* Valuing different ways of thinking

* Facilitating discussion / meetings

* Practicing humility, empathy, reciprocity, and humor

* Sharing leadership

* Conflict resolution / problem solving

* Reflection / analysis / assessment

* Power and influencer analysis

* Knowing multiple languages (literally and figuratively)

* Collaboration

* Ability to negotiate delicate power dynamics

* Cultural competency – understanding different cultural viewpoints and working to overcome unconscious bias

* Understanding privilege/difference

* Object-oriented craft techniques

* Improvisation skills

* Transforming and re-claiming space

* Risk-taking

* Researching

* Creating / fostering convivial spaces

* Fundraising

* Curating

* Methods of radical pedagogy and participatory curriculum planning for egalitarian production of knowledge

* Systems thinking

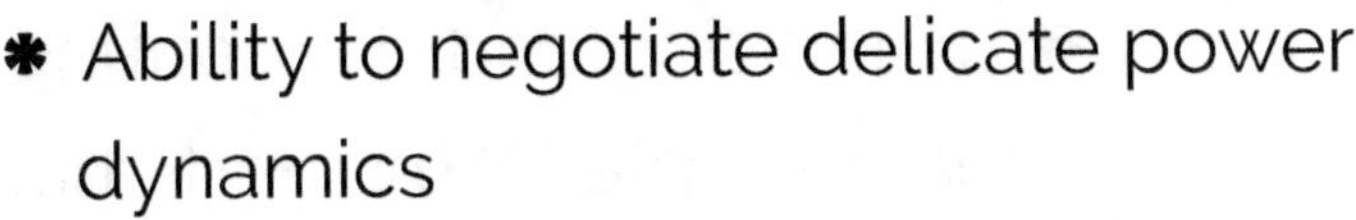

* Organizing and distributing content via multiple forms and channels for maximum access and to bypass gatekeepers

* Negotiating/Identifying intentions

* Methods of restorative justice

* Expressing appreciation

* Nonviolent resistance

* Relationship / partnership building / fostering trust

* Fostering agency in others

* Observational ability

* Facilitating decision making in diverse groups

* Creating and maintaining a collective

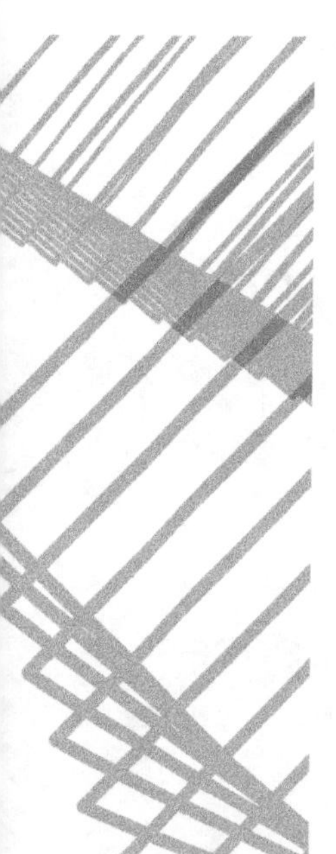

CREDITS:
1 > http://artmakingchange.org/
2 > http://artmakingchange.org/voices/the-minute-hand-of-social-engagement/
3 > http://studycollaboration.com/
4 > https://instructionalmoves.gse.harvard.edu/

SOME TIPS FOR EFFECTIVE SOCIAL PRACTICE

This is a collection of various ways to improve some social practice projects.

Not all the tips are applicable in all situations. Be thoughtful and considered in application. Remember that every social practice project is different.

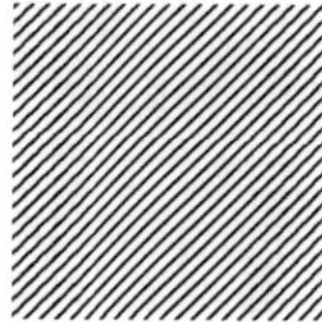

Secure an invitation to be there.

Be aware of your own bias and privilege.

Recognize and value local expertise, knowledge, and cultural practices.

Research and project-based learning are best pursued in the context of an actual site with social engagement.

Leave the community better than you found it (with new skills, resources, connections).

Practice creative, mindful, sustainable adaptive reuse of everything at hand as a means of being local.

Work with community-based entities (people or organizations) that can provide a through line for the work.

Find excitement in exploring alternatives to the way we research / work / live.

Practice reciprocity via genuine exchange and sharing of power between the artist and community at all stages of the process, from idea generation to aesthetic choices to implementation.

Consider connections between science, history, methods of living, environmental activism, and critical artistic practices. Practice generosity by recognizing that people's time and energy are precious, and making sure to provide something of real value in exchange.

Equitably compensate and recognize community members as co-creators.

Consider, "Reconfiguring our senses of ourselves and our work to focus on smaller, more autonomous, and more achievable outcomes." - Rick Prelinger in

"An Authentic Commons is Not a Temporary Affair"
(interview by Sarah Schultz & Sarah Peters)

As appropriate, consider helping people imagine the breadth of possibilities with some planned activities, and provide meeting space for new ideas/reflections to come to fruition.

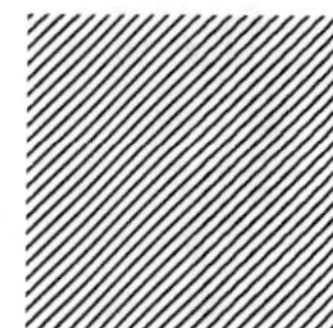

Dana DeMaster shares in greater detail the following tips in **How to Do Real Public Engagement** on StrongTowns.org:

Before holding a meeting [or starting a project]:
1. Build relationships before you need them.
2. Choose a neutral, accessible space.
3. Speak peoples' language.
4. Welcome children.

Adjust attitudes:
1. Engage people in the process from the beginning.
2. Provide a formal feedback loop.
3. Humanize the event.

CREDITS:
1 > http://artmakingchange.org
2 > http://www.mildredslane.com
3 > Sarah Schultz and Sarah Peters, editors. **Open Field: Conversation on the Commons**. Walker Art Center, 2012.

some
DISCUSSION
QUESTIONS
in social practice

1. How do places of intersubjective play and radical pedagogy produce different forms of collective behavior?

2. How is the media used as a form that resists dominant conditions of power?

3. What kinds of infrastructure can make social forms of play and politics?

4. How can we produce spaces where autonomous action is actually possible?

5. What type of city can we build using a hybrid of radical pedagogy and democratized play with the build environment?

6. How can we produce spaces and situations that upend ideas of race and class in a way that is fun, strange, and liberating?

Thompson, Nato, "Growing Dialogue: What is the Effectiveness of Socially Engaged Art?", in **Public Serv-ants**, ed. Burton, Johanna, Shannon Jackson, Dominic Willsdon, (Cambridge: The MIT Press, 2016), 446.

1. Is activism really important to the practice of socially engaged art?

2. Are artists inherently activists by practicing SEA?

Lowe, Rick, "Growing Dialogue: What is the Effectiveness of Socially Engaged Art?", in **Public Serv-ants**, ed. Burton, Johanna, Shannon Jackson, Dominic Willsdon, (Cambridge: The MIT Press, 2016), 453.

1. How does art impact the political and civic landscape?

2. What are the mechanics of cultural change?

3. What is political practice?

4. What's the difference between representing a political idea and enacting political change?

5. Is there such a thing as a liberatory form of art, or are the politics of art always a function of its intention or content?

6. Can artists change the world?What does that mean? Should they? How and how much?

7. If an artist can change the world, can I? Can we measure this type of change? Does it happen accidentally or on purpose? Is changing the world good art? How do we see it as art? What is its form? How does it circulate and generate a discourse around itself? Is it possible to support it using the art world's existing relationship to wealth?

Fisher, Deborah. "Evolving the Institution," in **Future Imperfect: A Blade of Grass.** *(A Blade of Grass Books, 2017)*

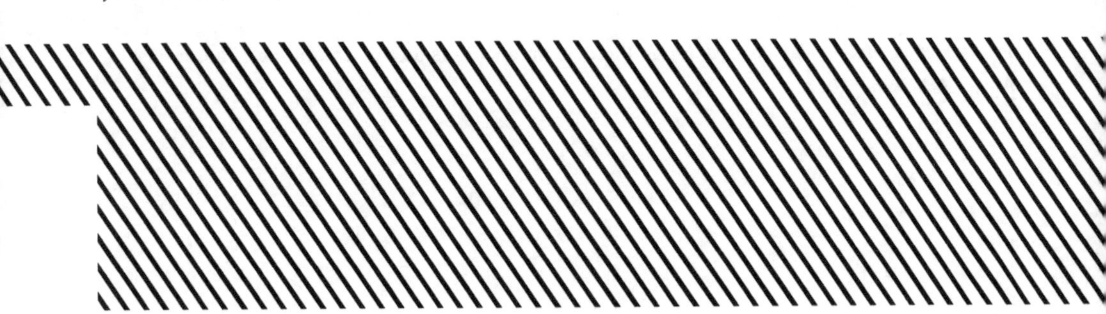

1. What does it mean to live a generative or creative public life?

2. How can we be more present with and for each other?

3. Gifting rather than owning?

4. Curiosity rather than certainty

5. Generosity rather than arrogance

6. Why do you think the idea of the commons has so much resonance now?

7. What does it mean to be a good cultural citizen?

8. What are the central moral and ethical tenets of free speech and assembly?

9. Who should be able to gather, to speak, to be here?

10. What exactly do we mean by "the public good"?

11. What do we do if they make bad art?

12. What if the activities aren't art at all?

Schultz, Sarah, and Sarah Peters, ed. **Open Field: Conversations on the Commons.** *Minneapolis: Walker Art Center, 2012.*

100 more questions available in
The Questions We Ask Together
compiled by Open Engagement.

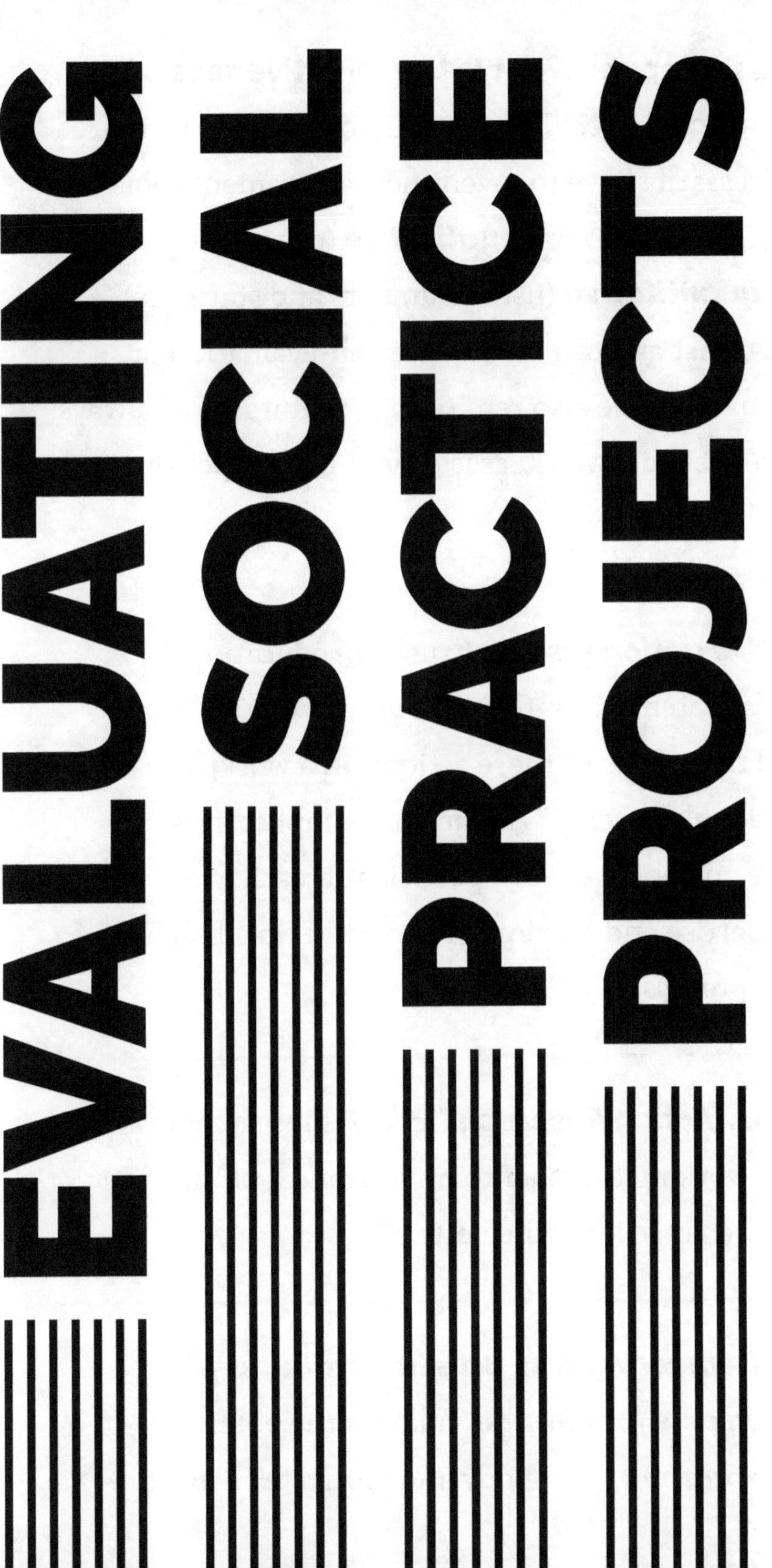

EVALUATING
SOCIAL
PRACTICE
PROJECTS

In **Growing Dialogue: What is the Effectiveness of Socially Engaged Art?**[1] Elizabeth Grady reminds us that we don't necessarily have to invent new assessment tools for socially engaged art. Several *qualitative* (descriptive with words) and *quantitative* (using numbers and statistics) tools already exist and can be used for self-evaluation or outside evaluation. She also reminds us, that it is not "always possible to assess such work; assessment is an expensive proposition"

Collaborative action research, used in educational settings, is "a systematic, reflective study of one's actions, and the effects of these actions, in a workplace or organizational context."[2] As the name implies, it is collaborative and engages each participant, each with different expertise and a unique perspective, in all phases of the research process.

Participatory Action Research "involves researchers and participants working together to understand a problematic situation and change it for the better."[3]

Animating Democracy's 11 artistic attributes of excellence in arts for change "address the potency of creative expression to embody and motivate change.

Aesthetic Perspectives aims to inform and inspire reflection, dialogue, and rich description in use by artists, funders, evaluators, educators, critics, presenters, programmers, curators, and audiences."[4] The attributes include

- >> risk-taking
- >> openness
- >> emotional experience
- >> sensory experience
- >> commitment
- >> communal meaning
- >> cultural integrity
- >> disruption
- >> coherence
- >> resourcefulness
- >> stickiness

This framework "elevates aesthetics in civically and socially engaged art, helps describe and assess the work, expands criteria for considering aesthetics in Arts for Change, addresses historical domination of Euro-American aesthetic standards, and promotes deeper appreciation of the rigor required for effective creative work."[5]

Ethnography "is a research method central to knowing the world from the standpoint of its social relations. It is a qualitative research method predicated on the diversity of culture at home (wherever that may be) and abroad. Ethnography involves hands-on, on-the-scene learning — and it is relevant wherever people are relevant."[6]

Sociological approaches include ***Macrosociological analysis*** (looking at the "big picture" that includes historical change over dozens or hundreds of years, such as the rise and fall of political systems or class hierarchies); ***Microsociological analysis*** (looking at the one-to-one interactions between individuals); ***Network analysis*** (examining the patterns of social ties among people in a group, and what those patterns mean for the group as a whole).[7]

Rick Lowe encourages evaluation of social practice in relationship to "power, privilege, appropriation, exploitation, etc." [8]

Jan Cohen-Cruz describes the following criteria for evaluation, as well as A Blade of Grass' values in, **The Imagination and Beyond: Toward a Method of Evaluating Socially Engaged Art**, ***Future Imperfect*** (2014-15)

>> An active relationship with those who would otherwise be strictly an audience contributes to social purpose.

>> A participatory art-making process is often more useful in social contexts than finished work.

- >> Partnering with people whose expertise is related to the social context brings in what the artists do not know.

- >> Identifying impact from the points of view of all the key partners in keeping with socially engaged art's goals.

A Blade of Grass' values:

- >> Artistic excellence.
- >> Artists in leadership roles to promote social change.

- >> Relevance to the participating communities.

Sheetal Prajapati asks questions such as the following, in **The Questions We Ask Together** (Open Engagement, 2015):

- >> Whose or what history (or histories) should be considered?
- >> Whose perspectives on a given history are acknowledged and available? Whose are not?

- >> Which discipline's historical narratives do you prioritize?
- >> How does an initiator understand their own history in relationship to their practice or community?

Further questions are listed on page 219, and Prajapati goes on to outline four considerations: power and the personal, responsibility, medium, and ethics as topics of consideration.

Claire Doherty lays out multiple lists of evaluative questions, such as the following in, in **The Questions We Ask Together** (Open Engagement, 2015), pages 266-267:

» Is it exploratory?

» Is it well-constructed?

» Does it provoke new and surprising encounters?

» Does it enable social interaction, or provoke new connections?

CREDITS:

1 > Grady, Elizabeth, "Growing Dialogue: What is the Effectiveness of Socially Engaged Art?", in **Public Servants**, ed. Burton, Johanna, Shannon Jackson, Dominic Willsdon, (Cambridge: The MIT Press, 2016), 441.

2 > http://cadres.pepperdine.edu/ccar/define.html

3 > http://www.participatorymethods.org/glossary/participatory-action-research

4 > http://www.animatingdemocracy.org/aesthetic-perspectives

5 > http://www.animatingdemocracy.org/aesthetic-perspectives

6 > https://anthropology.princeton.edu/research-programs/ethnographic-studies/what-ethnography

7 > https://www.dummies.com/education/science/types-of-sociological-analysis/

8 > Lowe, Rick, "Growing Dialogue: What is the Effectiveness of Socially Engaged Art?", in **Public Servants**, ed. Burton, Johanna, Shannon Jackson, Dominic Willsdon, (Cambridge: The MIT Press, 2016), 446.

Intersection of
CRAFT
and
SOCIAL PRACTICE

There is a long history of craft intersecting with prominent themes in our current understanding of social practice. Craft has often highlighted "...questions of collectivity, civil systems, and underlying meanings instigated and produced by communal gatherings." Some trends visible at the intersection of craft and social practice include:

THE ACT OF CRAFTING TOGETHER

This practice is inherently social when we look at historical instances of knitting, quilting, and embroidery groups, or even craft practices related to food such as canning, gardening, or crafting a group meal. What other craft practices can you think of that fit this category?

USING CRAFTED OBJECTS TO FACILITATE CONVERSATION

Ceramics and glass might at first seem to be the most prominent materials in this category, as they lend themselves to utilitarian food-oriented objects such as tea sets, wine glasses, and other dishwares

continued ⇥

Using crafted objects...

which help facilitate eating together. However, furniture making can also be central for facilitating conversation. What other craft practices can you think of that fit this category?

CRAFTIVISM

Crafting with a specific political intention. A recent example is the knitted pussyhat from the 2016 U.S. election. This practice is interesting because it allowed people to participate in a group endeavor from afar, in groups, or in isolation.

CREDITS:

1 > Gupta Wiggers, Namita. "Socialization vs. Social Objects." **Social Objects**, by Socially Engaged Craft Collective (2017).

A SOCIAL PRACTICE BOOK LIST

A list of books related to understanding, practicing, and thinking about public and social practice.

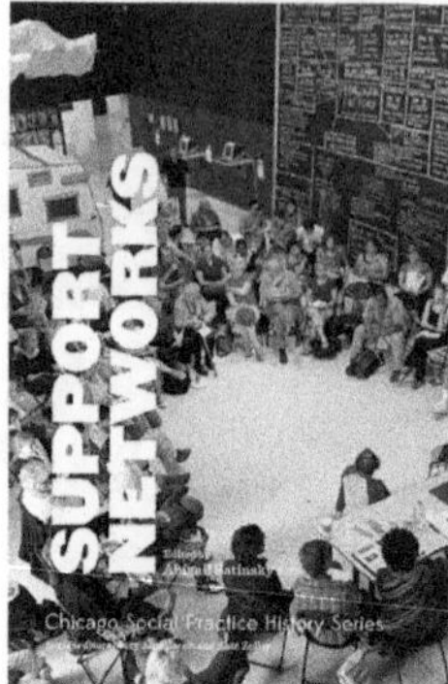

Support Networks

Satinsky, Abigail

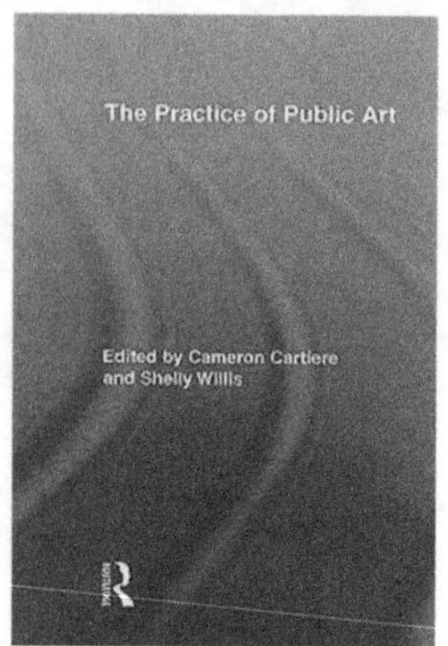

The Practice of Public Art

Cartiere and **Willis, eds.**

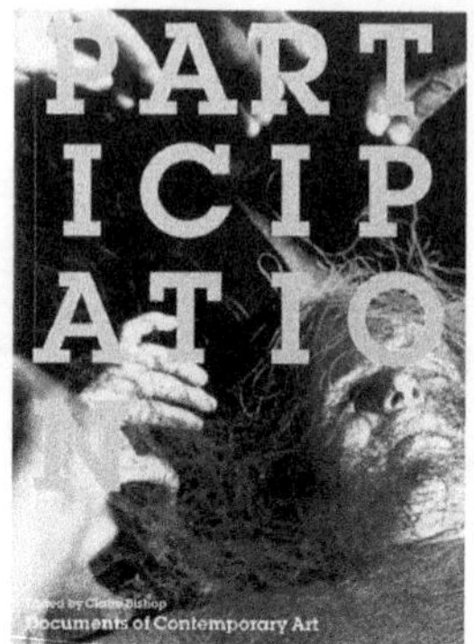

Participation

Bishop,Claire

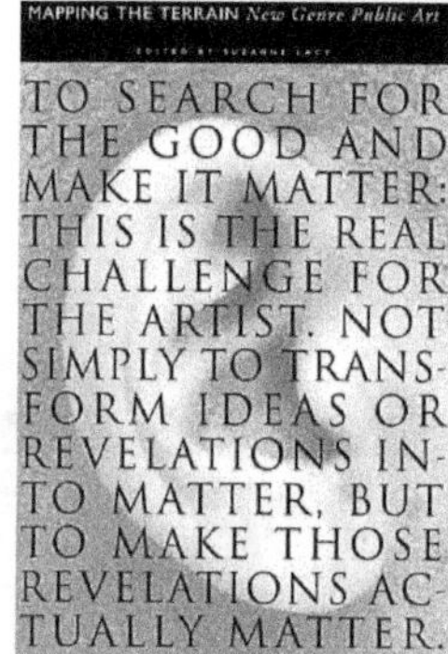

Mapping the Terrain: New Genre Public Art

Lacy, Suzanne

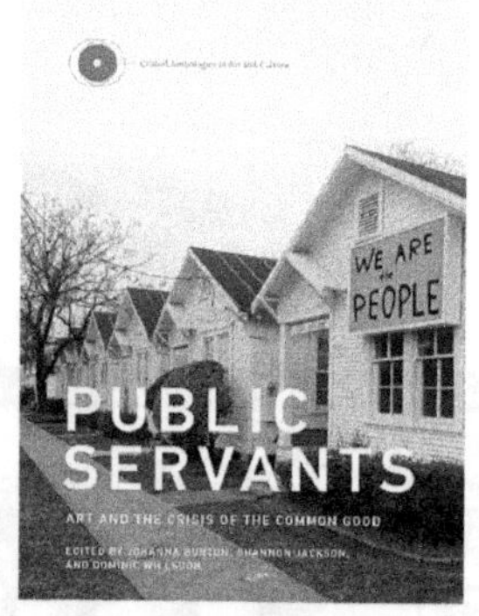

Public Servants: Art and the Crisis of the Common Good

Burton, Jackson and **Willsdon**

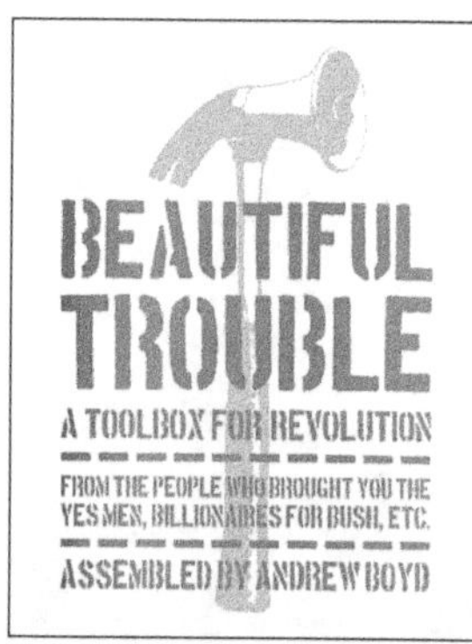

Beautiful Trouble: A Toolbox for Revolution

Boyd and **Mitchell**

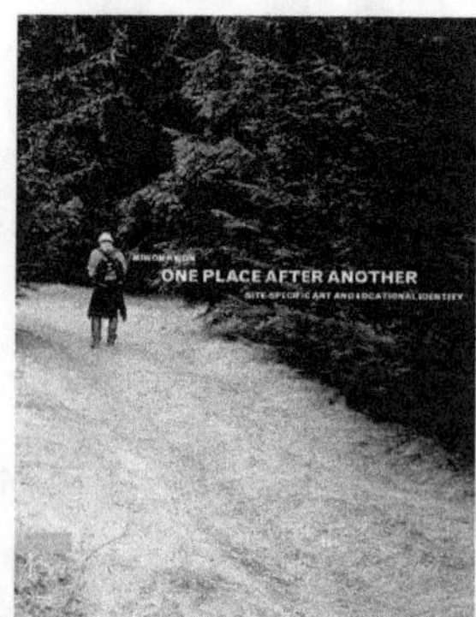

One Place after Another: Site-Specific Art and Locational Identity

Kwon , Miwon

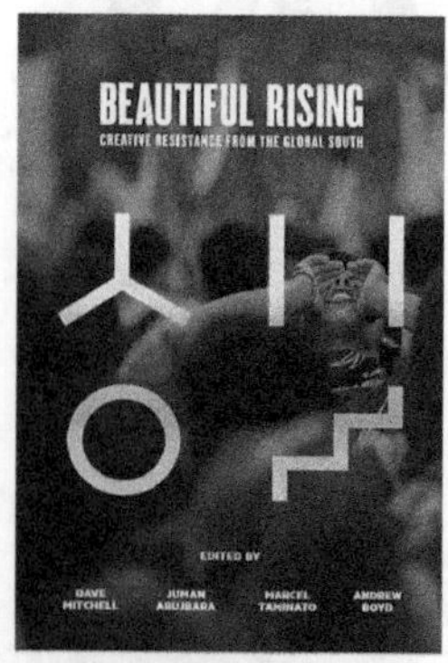

Beautiful Rising: Creative Resistance From The Global South

Abujbara, Boyd, Mitchell, and **Taminato**

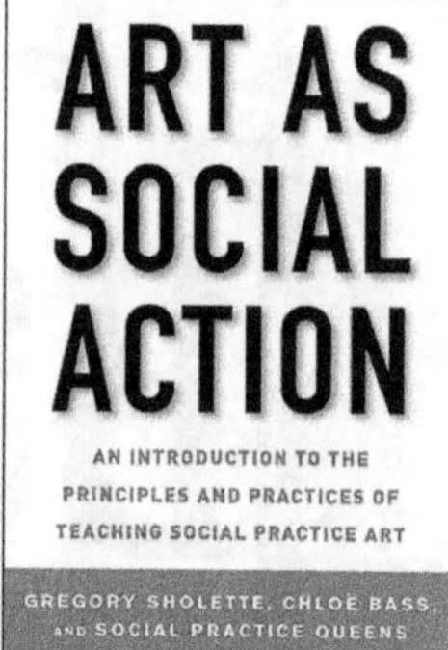

Art as Social Action: An Introduction to the Principles and Practices of Teaching Social Practice Art

Sholette and **Bass**

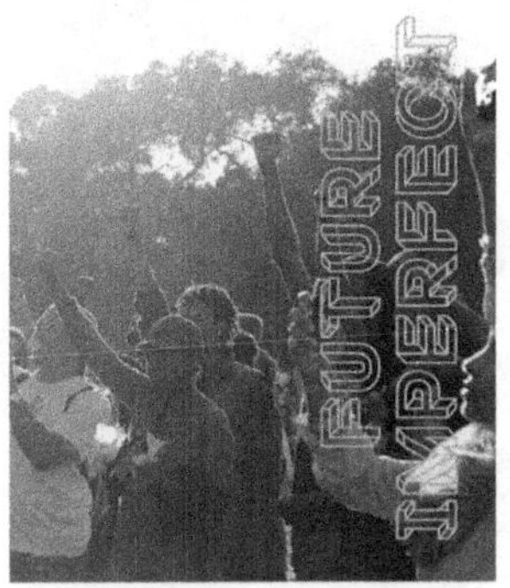

Future Imperfect

Grady, Elizabeth

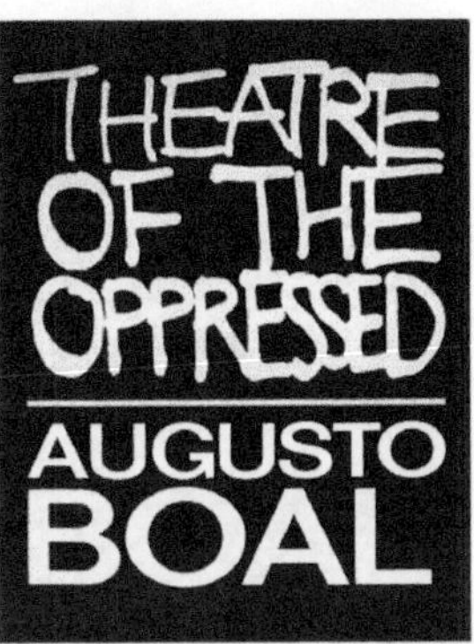

Theatre of the Oppressed

Boal, Augusto

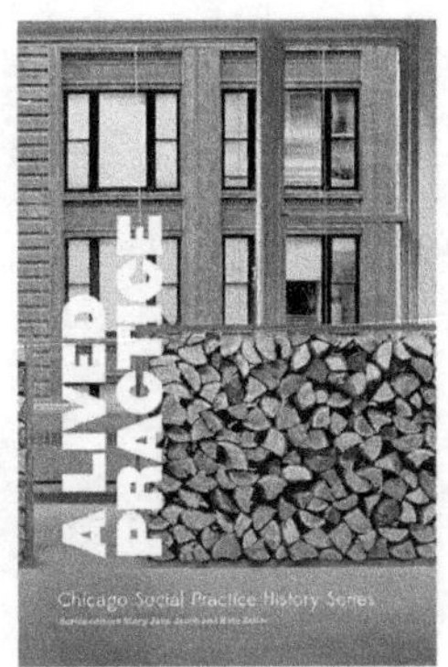

A Lived Practic

Jacob, Mary Jane

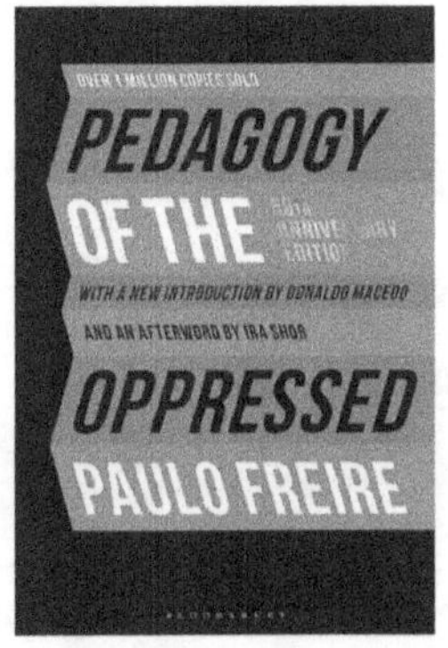

Pedagogy of the Oppressed (50th Anniversary ed.)

Freire, Paulo

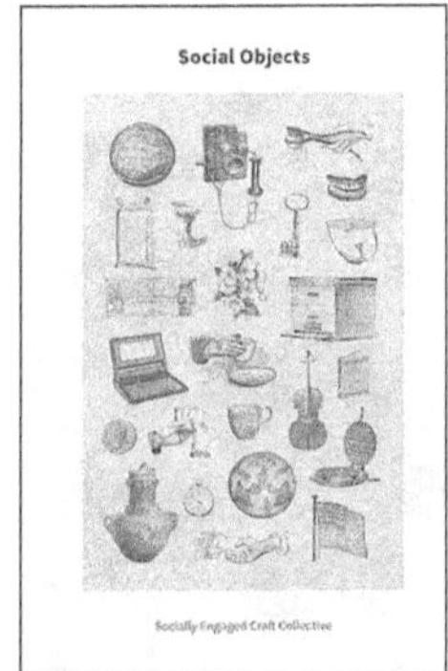

Social Objects

Socially Engaged Craft Collective, ed.

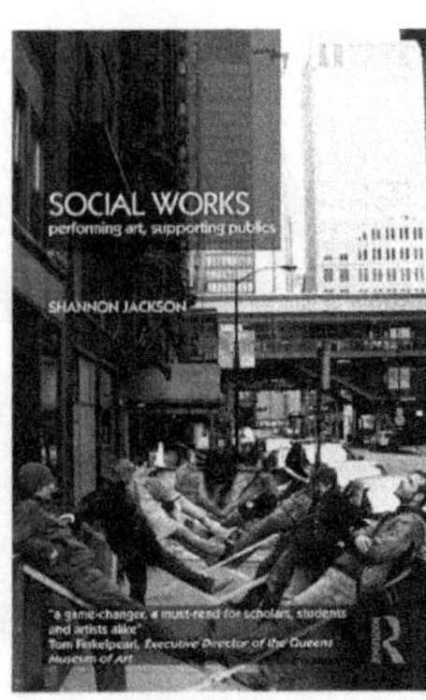

Social Works: Performing Art, Supporting Publics

Jackson, Shannon

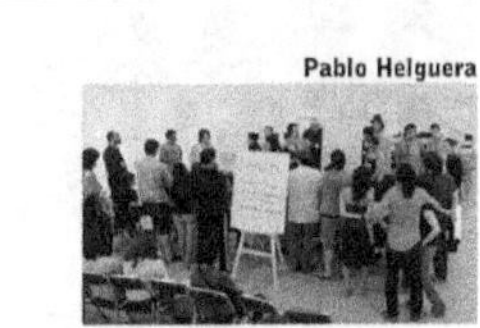

Education for Socially Engaged Art: A Materials and Techniques Handbook

Helguera, Pablo

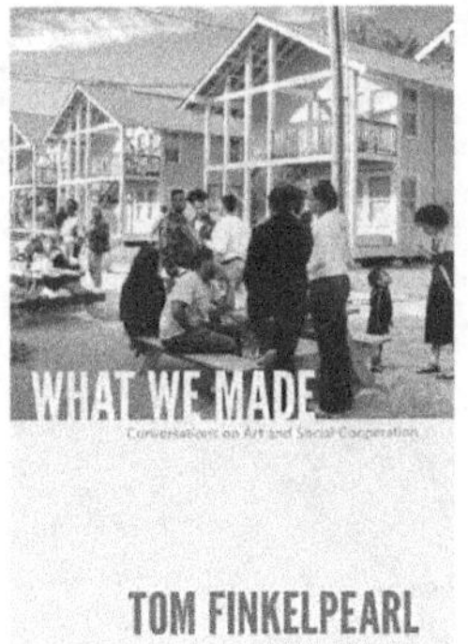

What We Made: Conversations on Art and Social Cooperation

Finkelpearl, Tom

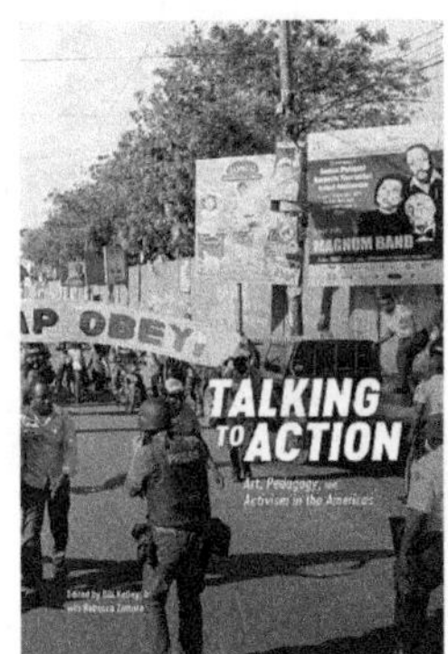

Talking to Action: Art, Pedagogy, and Activism in the Americas

Kelly, Jr., Bill

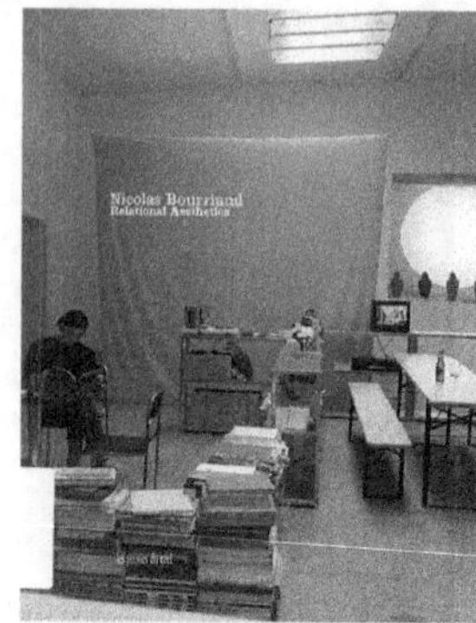

Relational Aesthetics

Bourriaud, Nicolas

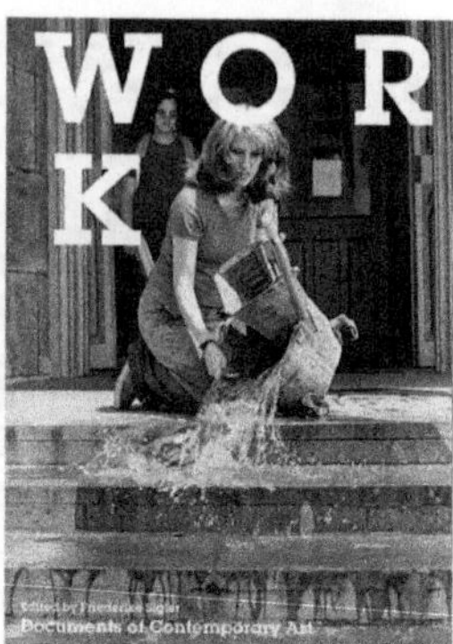

Work

Sigler, Friederike ed.

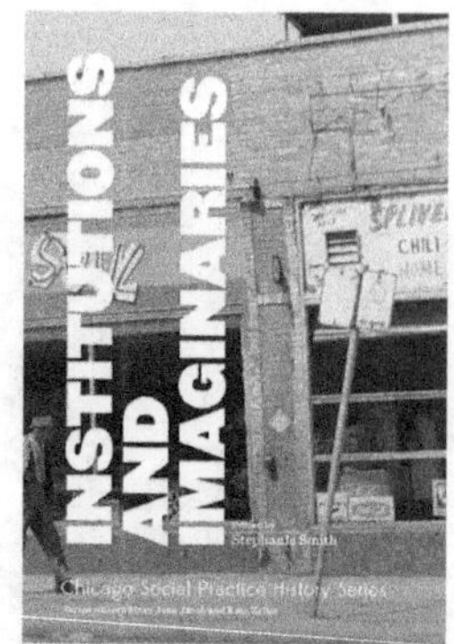

Institutions and Imaginaries

Smith, Stephanie

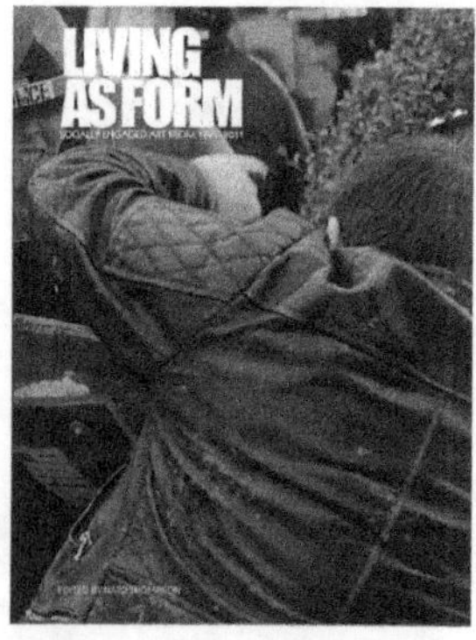

Living as Form: Socially Engaged Art from 1991–2011

Thompson, Nato

Seeing Power: Art and Activism in the 21st Century

Thompson, Nato

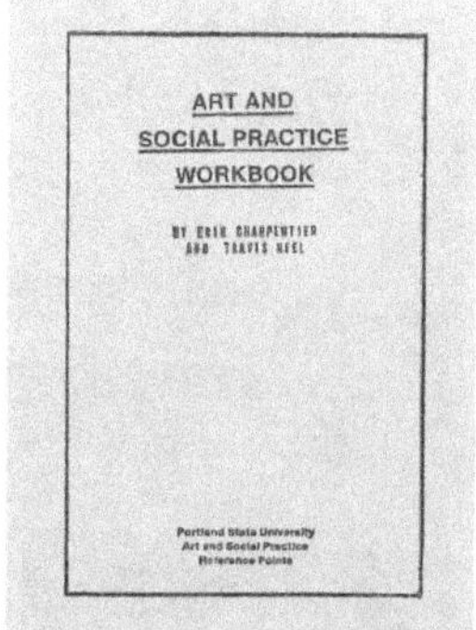

Art and Social Practice Workbook

Charpentier and **Neel**

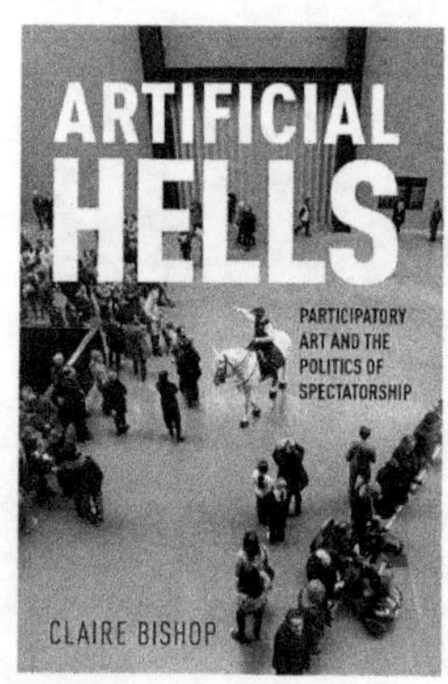

Artificial Hells: Participatory Art and the Politics of Spectatorship

Bishop, Claire

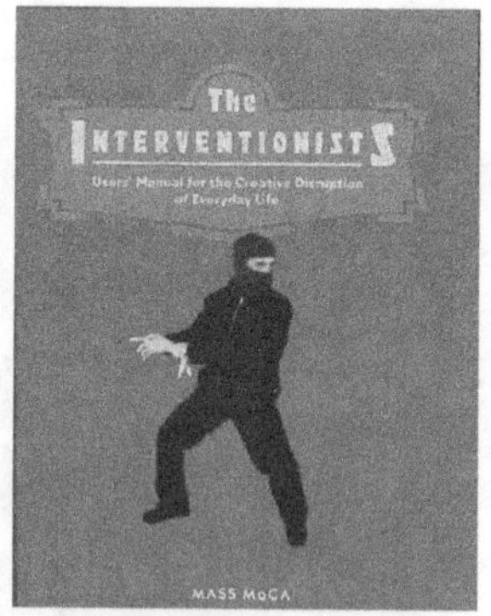

The Interventionists: Users' Manual for the Creative Disruption of Everyday Life

Thompson and **Sholette**

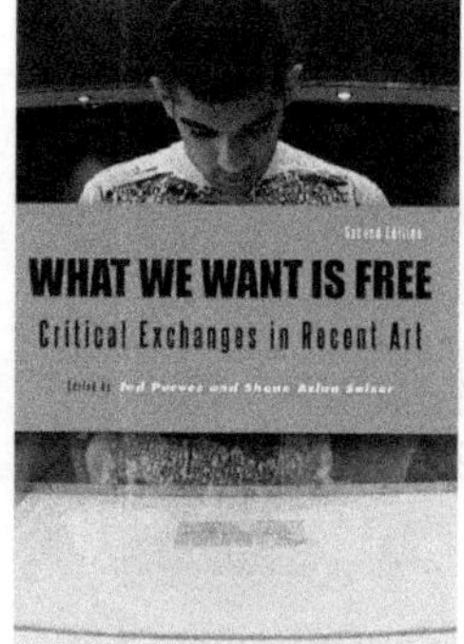

What We Want Is Free: Critical Exchange in Recent Art

Purves and **Selzer**

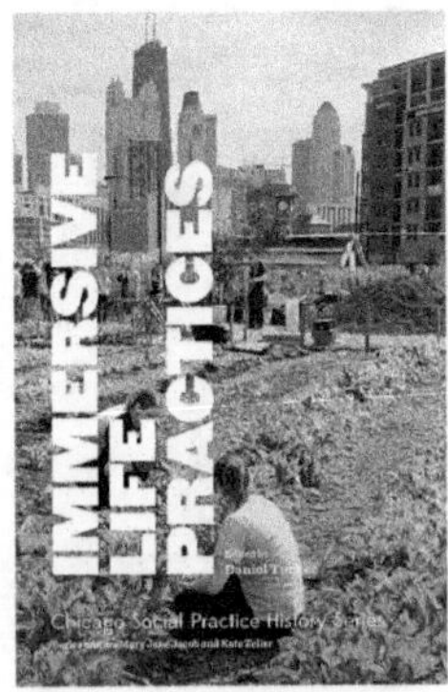

Immersive Life Practices

Tucker, Daniel

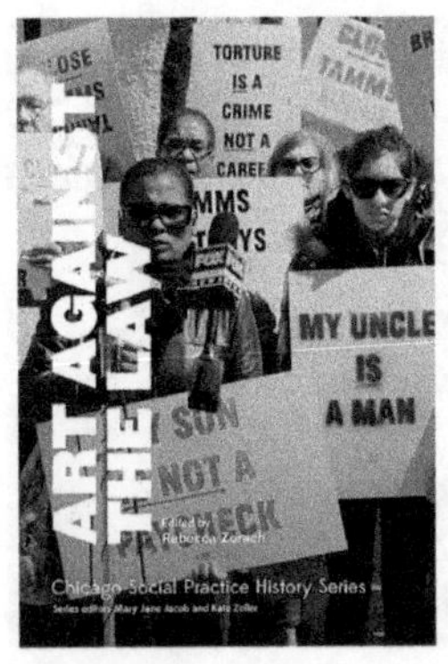

Art Against the Law

Zorach, Rebecca

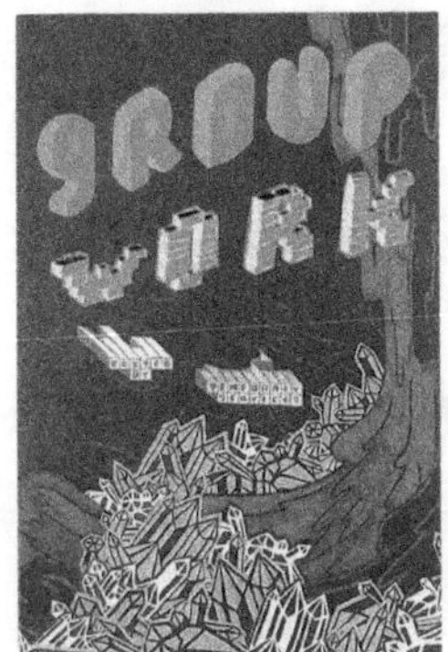

Group Work

Temporary Services, ed.

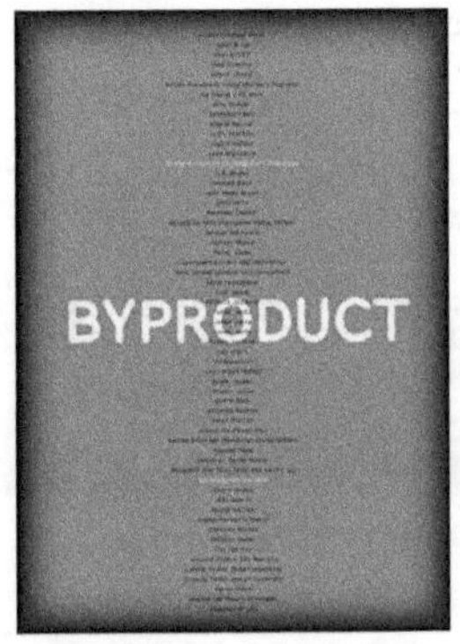

Byproduct: On the Excess of Embedded Art Practices

Jahn, Marisa ed.

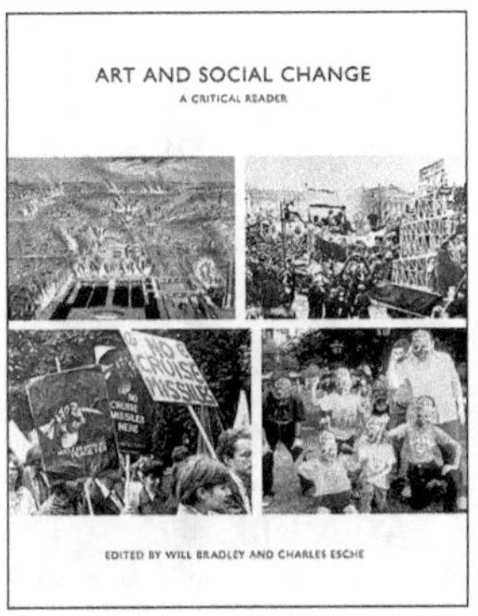

Art and Social Change, A Critical Reader

Bradley and **Esche**, ed.

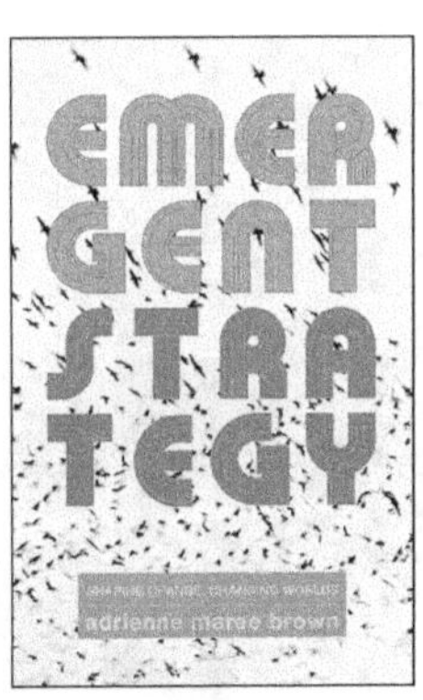

Emergent Strategy: Shaping Change, Changing Worlds

brown, adrienne maree

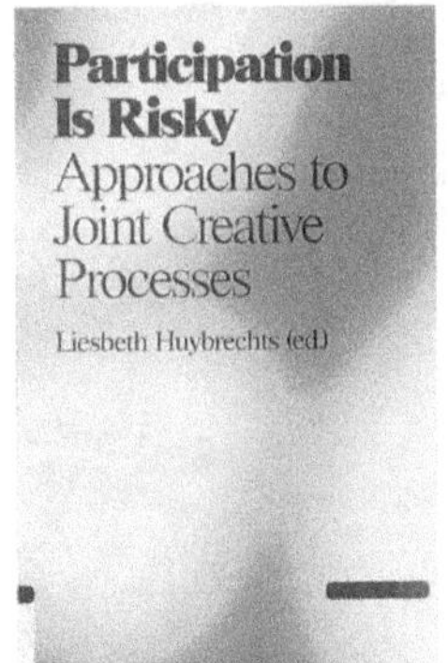

Participation Is Risky: Approaches to Joint Creative Processes

Schepers, Schoffelen, Lee, Storni, and **Huybrechts**

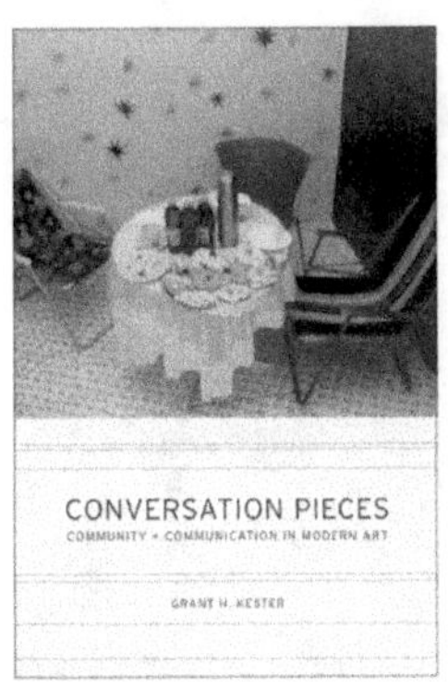

Conversation Pieces: Community and Communication in Modern Art

Kester, Grant H

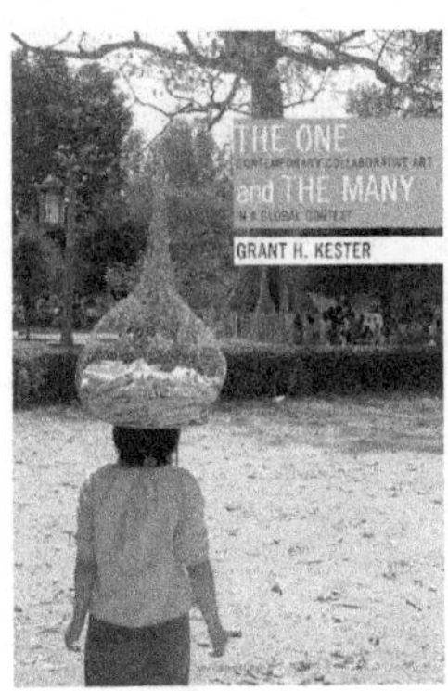

The One and the Many: Contemporary Collaborative Art in a Global Context

Kester, Grant H

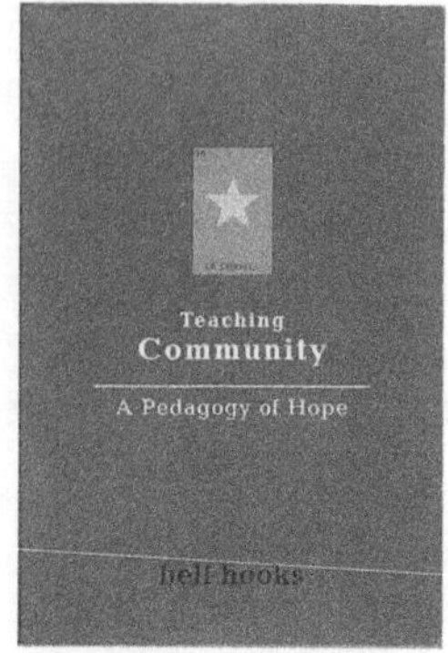

Teaching Community

bell hooks

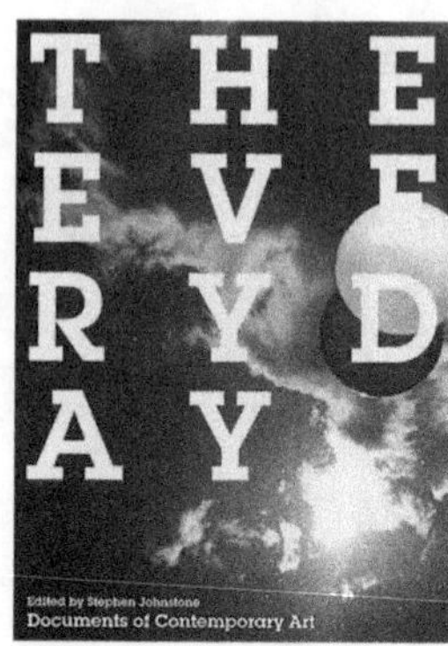

The Everyday

Johnstone, Stephen, ed.

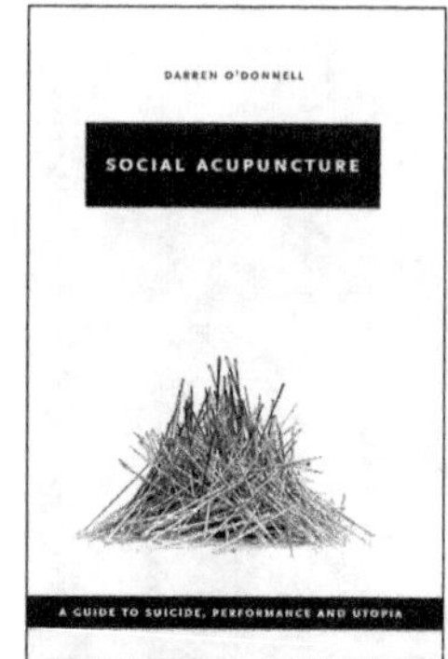

Social Acupuncture

O'Donnell, Darren

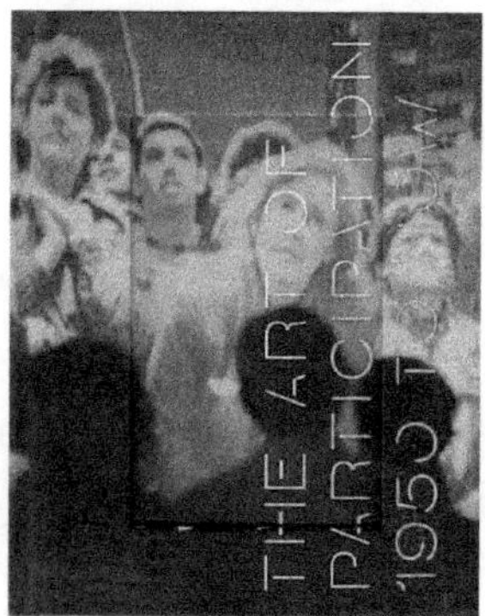

The Art of Participation, 1950–Now

Frieling, Rudolph

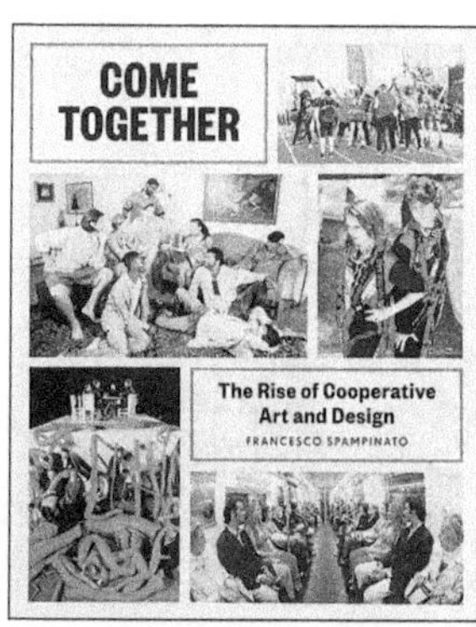

Come Together: The Rise of Cooperative Art and Design

Spampinato, Francesco

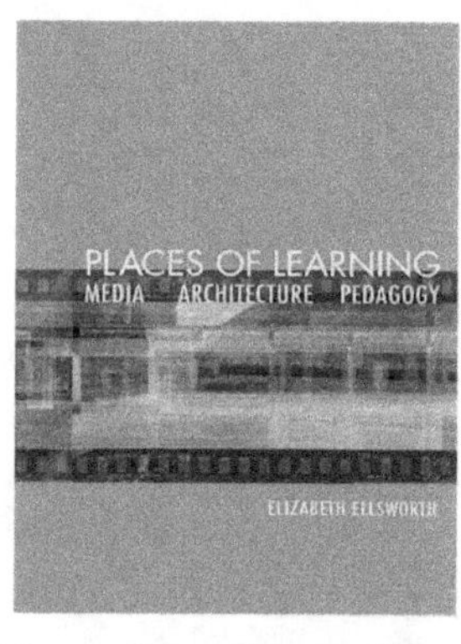

Places of Learning, Media, Architecture, Pedagogy

Ellsworth, Elizabeth

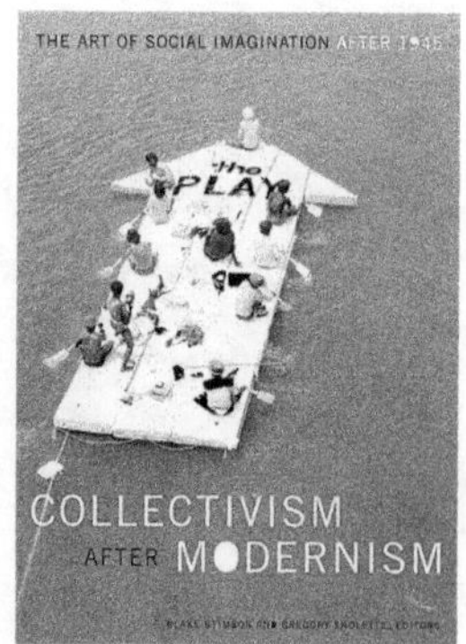

Collectivism After Modernism, The Art of Social Imagination After 1945

Stimson and **Sholette**, ed.

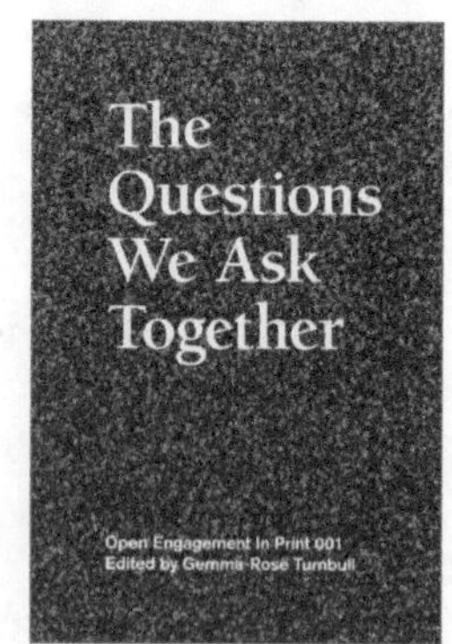

The Questions We Ask Together

Turnbull, Gemma-Rose, ed.

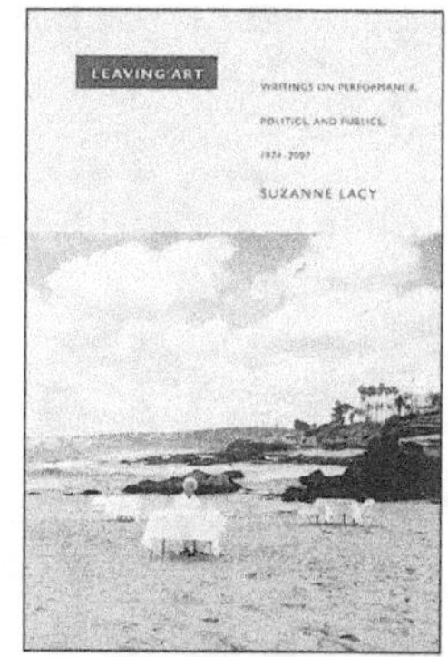

Leaving Art: Writings on Performance, Politics, and Publics, 1974–2007

Lacy, Suzanne

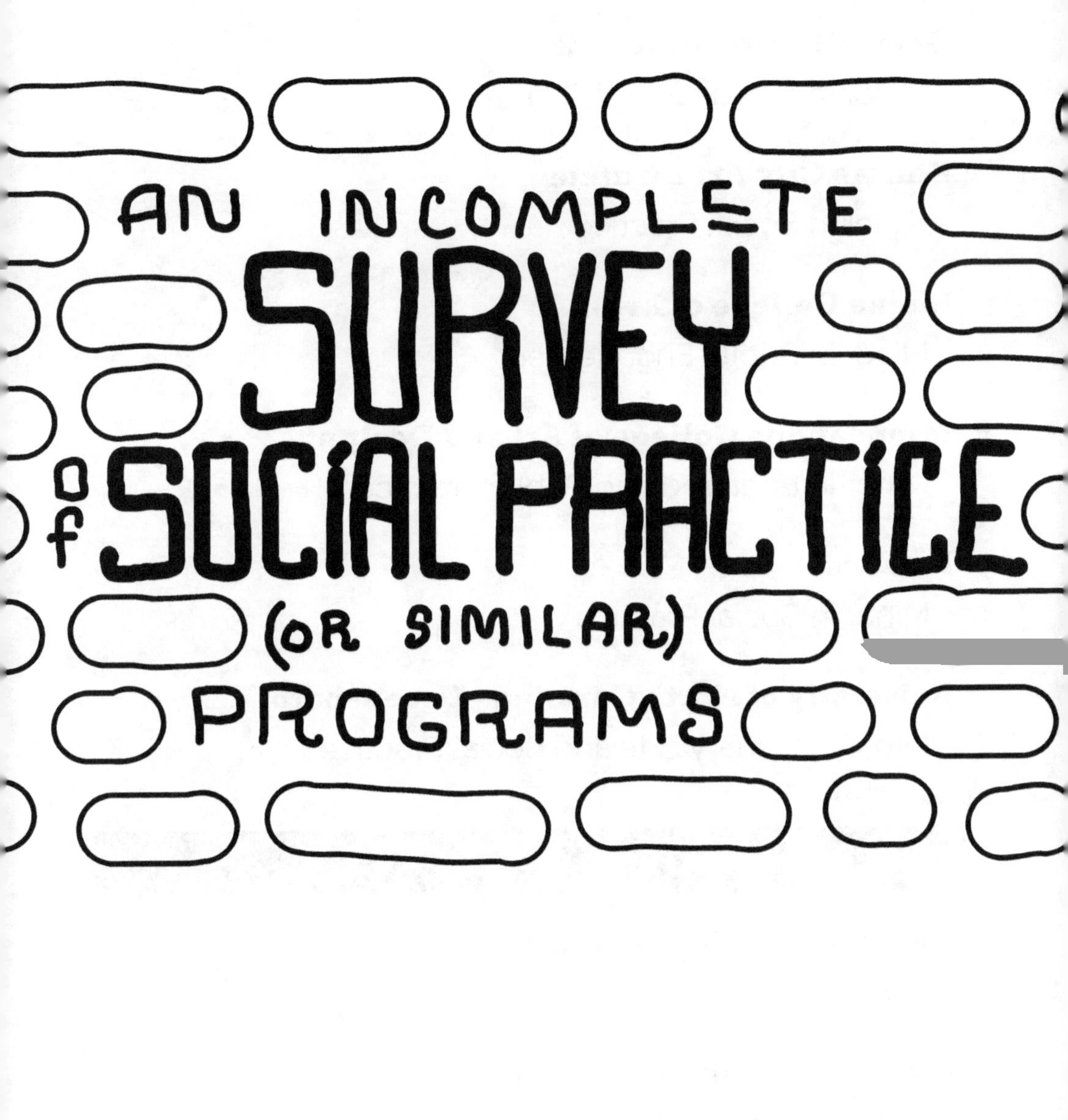

AN INCOMPLETE
SURVEY
OF SOCIAL PRACTICE
(OR SIMILAR)
PROGRAMS

MINORS:

George Mason University
Minor in Arts as Social Change

Kansas City Art Institute
Minor in Social Practice

Maine College of Art
Minor in Public Engagement

Minneapolis College of Art and Design
Minor in Engaged and Public Practices

Parsons
Minor in Social Practice

University of North Carolina - Greensboro
Interdisciplinary Arts and Social Practice

UNDERGRADUATE:

California College of the Arts
BFA in Community Arts

Emily Carr University of Art and Design
BFA in Critical and Cultural Practices

Maryland Institute College of Art
BFA studio concentration in Sustainability & Social Practice

University of Minnesota

BFA in Art - Interdisciplinary Art and Social Practice

Wichita State University

BFA in Art - Studio Art: Community & Social Practices
Concentration

GRADUATE:

Bennington College

MFA in Public Action

California College of the Arts

MA in Social Practice and Public Forms

Maryland Institute College of Art

MFA in Community Arts

Moore College of Art & Design

MFA/MA in Socially Engaged Art

National College of Art and Design, Dublin

MA in Socially Engaged Art + Further Education

New York University

MA in Art, Education, and Community Practice

Nomad

Interdisciplinary MFA

Northeastern University

MFA in Interdisciplinary Arts, emphasis in the arts of
engagement

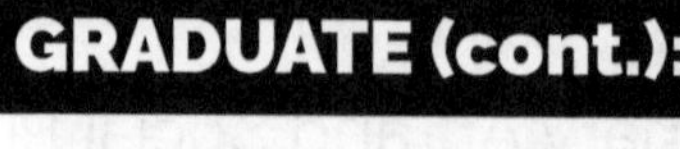

GRADUATE (cont.):

Otis College of Art and Design
MFA in Social Practice Art

Parsons
MA in Theories of Urban Practice / MFA in Transdisciplinary Design

Portland State University
MFA in Art and Social Practice

School of Visual Arts
MFA in Design for Social Innovation

Social Practice Queens
MFA

University of Indianapolis
MA in Social Practice Art

University of Minnesota
MFA in Art - Interdisciplinary Art and Social Practice

University of Pennsylvania
MSW / MFA Dual Degree

OTHER PROGRAMS:

Social Practice Queens
Certificate

Some SOCIAL PRACTICE HISTORY

EARLY 1900s

The history of social practice includes elements of art, social justice, theatre, performance, music, politics, and more. It includes many artists, events, and projects not mentioned here. Here are some **manifestations of performance art near the beginning of the 1900s...**

FUTURISM

1909-1920s

These artists embraced **speed, dynamism, and a love of danger**, coupled with performance as a way to force audiences to confront these ideas. Everyone had a manifesto. Artists experimented with instructions on how to perform in order to liberate potential performers from old techniques. Some experimented with noise music, mechanical movements, and simultaneity.

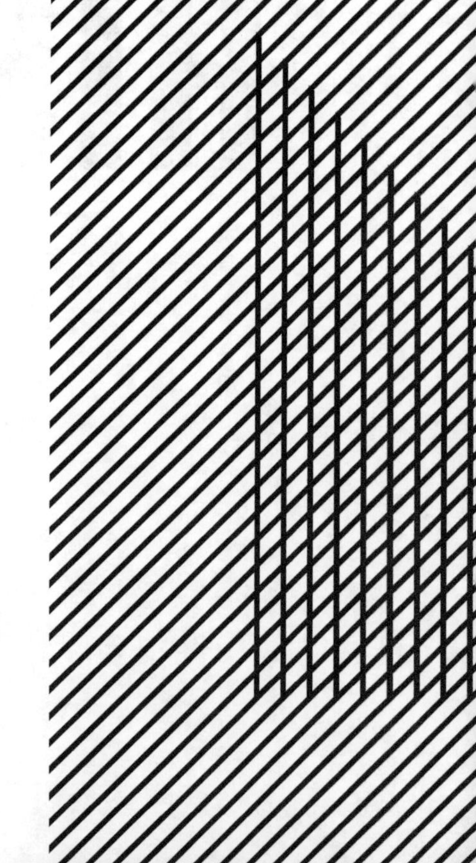

DADA

1916~1924

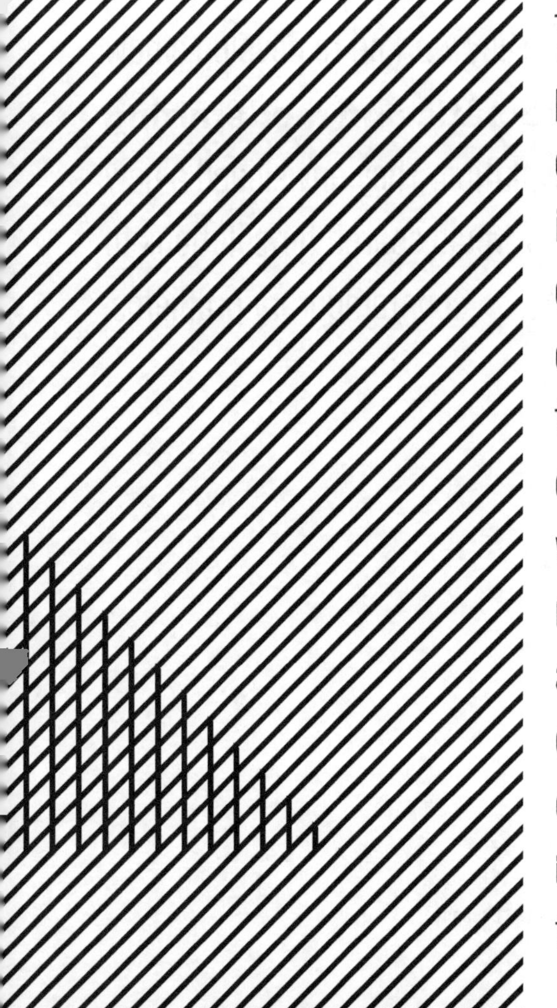

The Dada movement was a protest against the barbarism of World War I, middle-class interests, and oppressive expectations in both art and everyday society. Thus, some focused on simultaneity and chance. Cabaret Voltaire was founded for artists who rejected the logic, reason, and aestheticism of modern capitalist society, instead expressing **nonsense, irrationality, and protest** in their works.

RUSSIAN CONSTRUCTIVISM

1915-1930s

These artists desired to express the political views and the disorientation of modern life. They worked to develop a new form of **art for the democratic and modernizing goals** of the Russian Revolution. They envisioned a new society of cultural workers who would search for solutions to contemporary problems.

CREDITS:
1 > RoseLee Goldberg, **Performance Art: From Futurism to the Present**
2 > http://www.theartstory.org/

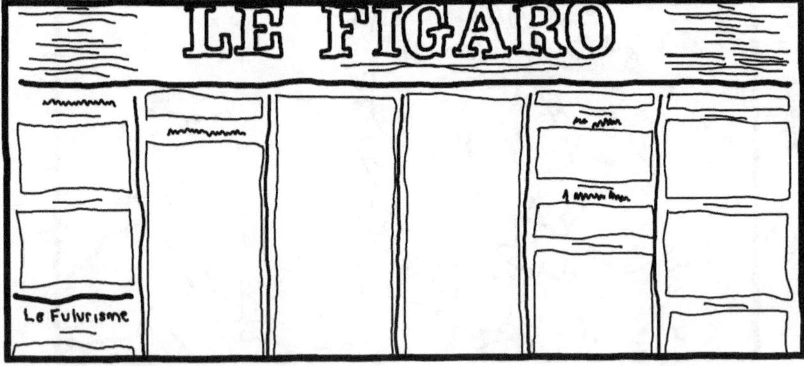

Filippo Tommaso Marinetti

Futurist Manifesto

1909

He wrote the first futurist manifesto, and it embraced love of speed and danger.

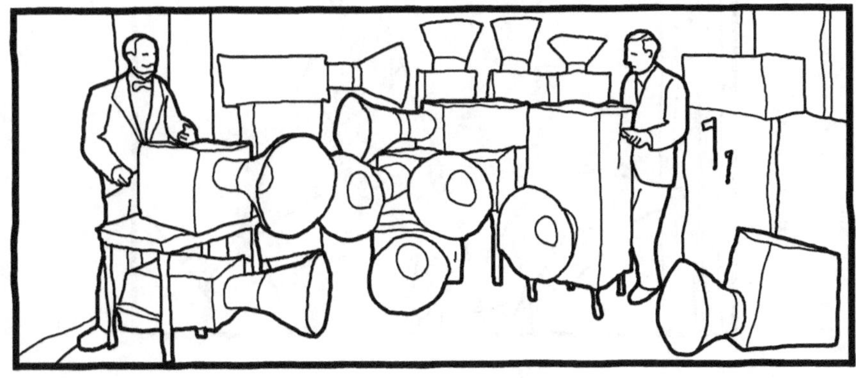

Luigi Russolo

Veglio Di Una Città

1913

He created noise instruments (intonarumori) and noise compositions.

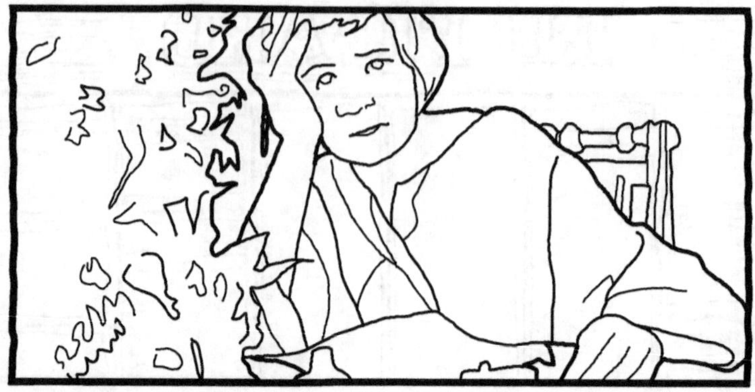

Emmy Hennings

Cabaret Voltaire

1916

She co-founded Cabaret Voltaire and was the only professional cabaret performer to perform there. She devised new works daily.

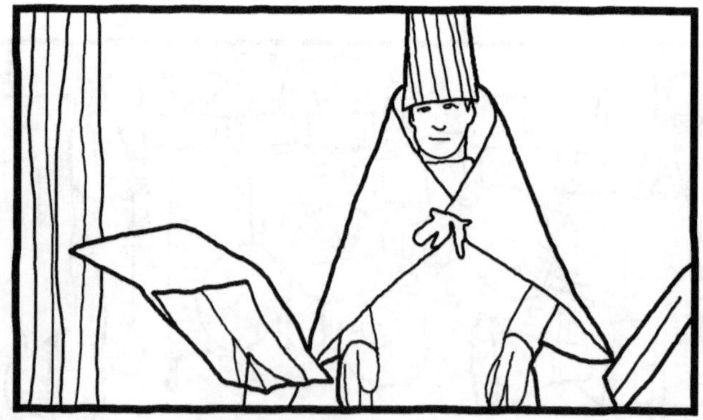

Hugo Ball

Karawane

1916

Among other projects, he wrote a randomized sound poem, *Karawane*, and co-founded Cabaret Voltaire.

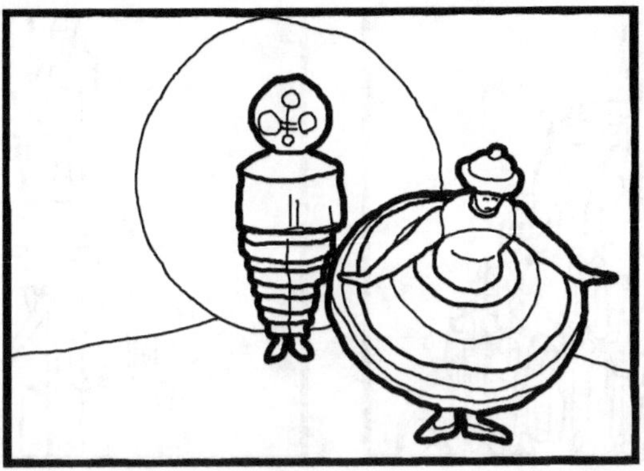

Oskar Schlemmer

Das triadische Ballet (The Triadic Ballet)

1916–22

Conceived of the human body as a new artistic medium, and called for complex movements and elaborate costumes.

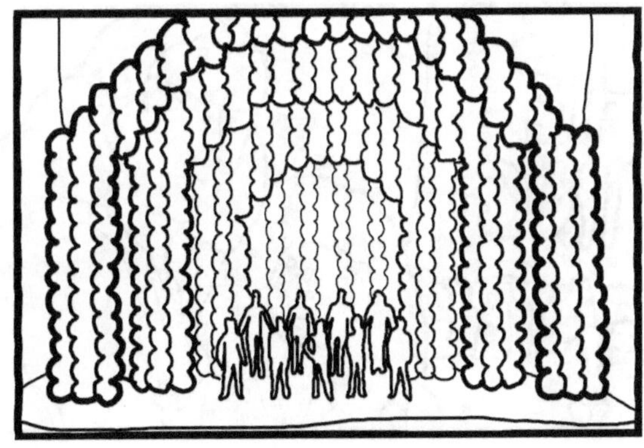

Francis Picabia

Relâche

1924

A ballet with music composed by Erik Satie. The title was thought to be a Dadaist joke because relâche means cancelled or closed in French.

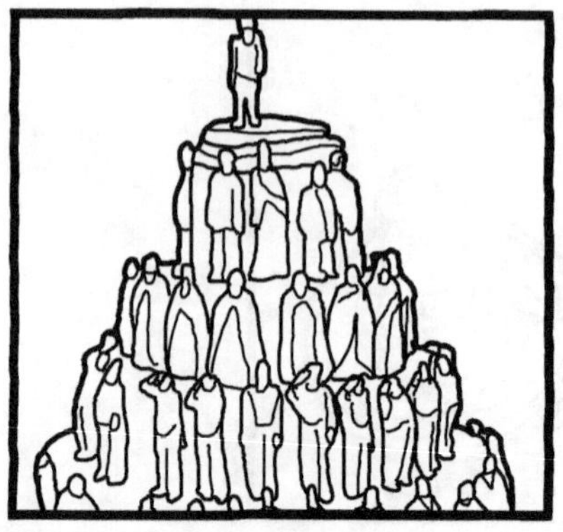 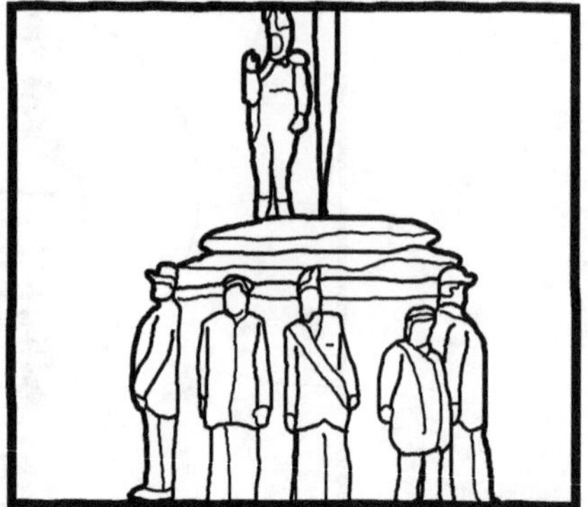

Vladamir Mayakovsky

Moscow is Burning

1930

This was a pantomime performance involving 500 performers and presented in the second half of a circus. It showcases political satire of the first days of the Revolution.

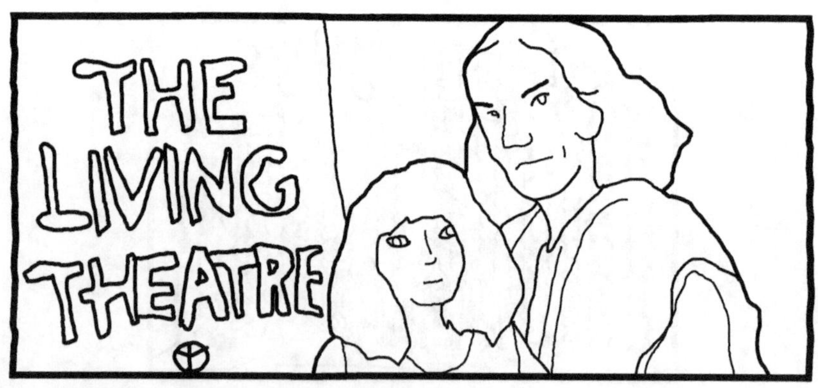

The Living Theatre

1947-2014

The Living Theatre was dedicated to transforming the organization of power within society from a competitive, hierarchical structure to cooperative and communal expression.

Some SOCIAL PRACTICE HISTORY

1950s

The history of social practice includes elements of art, social justice, theatre, performance, music, politics, and more. It includes many artists, events, and projects not mentioned here. Here are some **key events around the 1950s...**

CIVIL RIGHTS

1950s-1960s

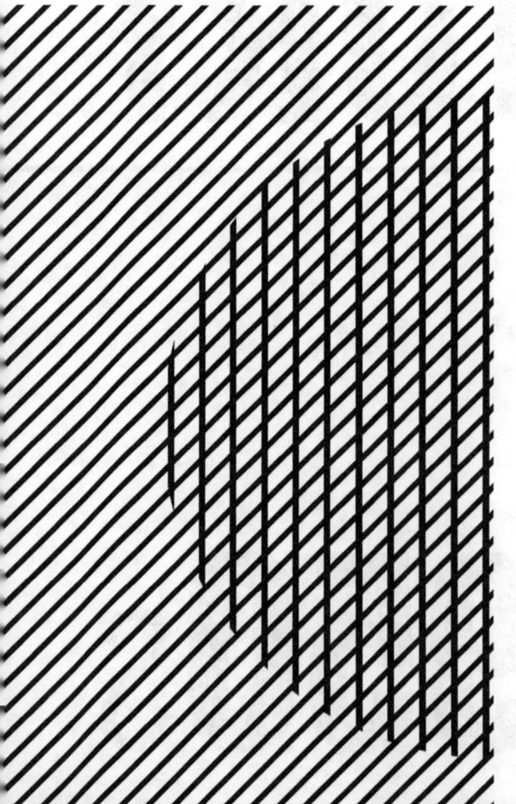

The civil rights movement was a **struggle for social justice** that took place mainly during the 1950s-1960s for Black people to gain **equal rights under the law** in the United States.

NEW FORMS THRIVE IN
JAPAN

JIKKEN KOBO
EXPERIMENTAL WORKSHOP   //   1951–1957

In Tokyo, Jikken Kobo, a **cross-disciplinary, intermedia art collective** of visual artists, composers, photographers, musicians, designers, writers and others were experimenting with cross-discipline presentations. Working between 1951 and 1957, For many, the group signaled the **rebirth of avant-garde art** in **postwar Japan**.

GUTAI BIJUTSU KYOKAI
GUTAI ARTIST ASSOCIATION   //   1954–1972

Founded by artist Yoshihara Jiro, they represented a radical approach to artmaking that encompassed **performance, painting, installation, and theatrical events**, taking advantage of the freedoms available in their newly democratic homeland. Gutai's early outdoor staged events sought to **break new ground between art and everyday life**. Members explored the boundaries of collective creativity and participation between artist and audience.

SITUATIONISM

1957-1972

The Situationists have often been cited as the **genesis of social practice**. They embraced **critique of capitalism and consumerism** as an **expression of identity**, versus directly lived experiences, or the first-hand fulfillment of authentic desires.

CREDITS:
1 > RoseLee Goldberg, **Performance Art: From Futurism to the Present**
2 > http://www.theartstory.org/

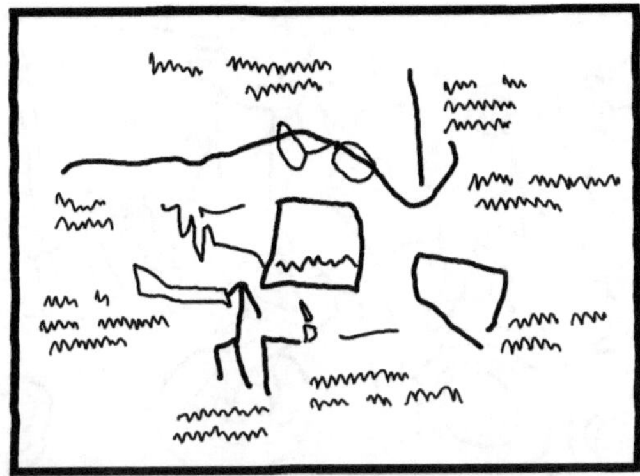

John Cage

Theatre Piece No . 1

1954 - Black Mountain College, North Carolina

This was an unscripted performance considered by many to be the first Happening. The event took place in the Black Mountain College dining hall and also included choreographer Merce Cunningham, pianist David Tudor and painter Robert Rauschenberg.

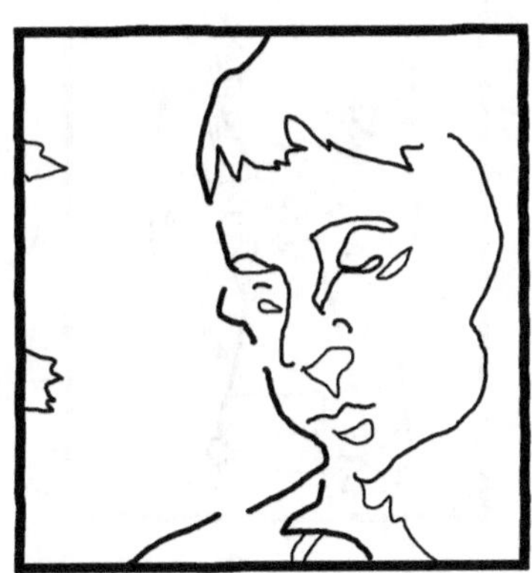

Guy Debord

Theory of the Derive

1958

A manual for psychogeographic procedures, executed through the act of derive ("drift"). Debord defines the dérive as "a mode of experimental behavior linked to the conditions of urban society: a technique of rapid passage through varied ambiances."

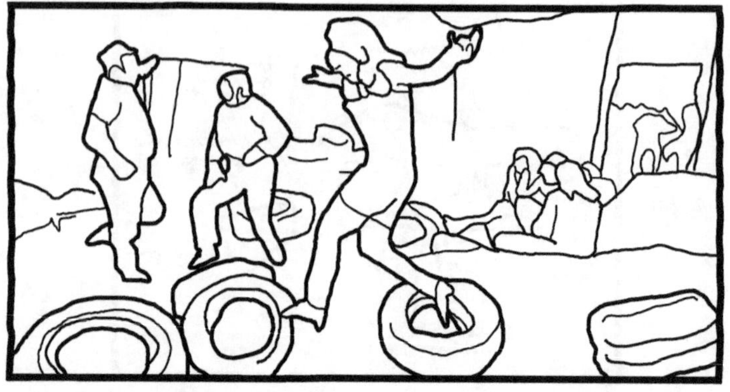

Allan Kaprow

18 Happenings in 6 Parts

1959

The public was invited to follow the directions from a score to create 'something spontaneous, something that just happens to happen.'

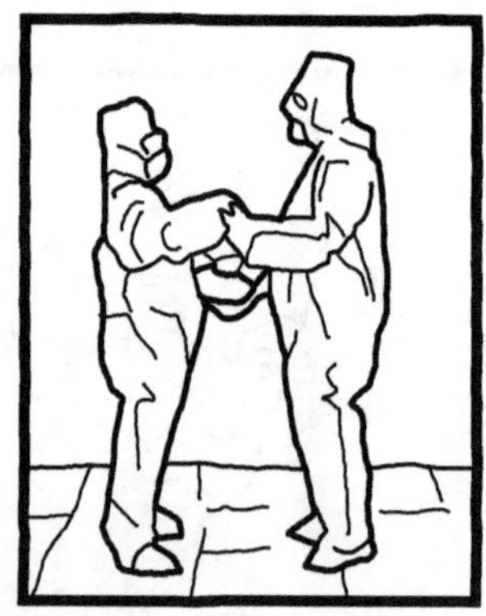

Lygia Clark and Helio Oiticica

Neo-Concretism

1959–61

This consisted of interactive & participatory works, such as Clark's ***O eu e o tu (The I and the you)*** from 1967, in which 2 rubber suits are joined by a tube, and the wearers are unable to see one another. Clark said of her pieces, "What's important is the act of doing in the present; the artist is dissolved into the world."

Some SOCIAL PRACTICE HISTORY

1960s

The history of social practice includes elements of art, social justice, theatre, performance, music, politics, and more. It includes many artists, events, and projects not mentioned here. Here are some **key events around the 1960s...**

SECOND-WAVE

FEMINISM

1960s

Influenced and inspired by the Civil Rights Movement, **organizations** were formed which **changed the way women viewed themselves and each other**, while also pursuing legislation designed to give women **equal opportunities** on par with men.

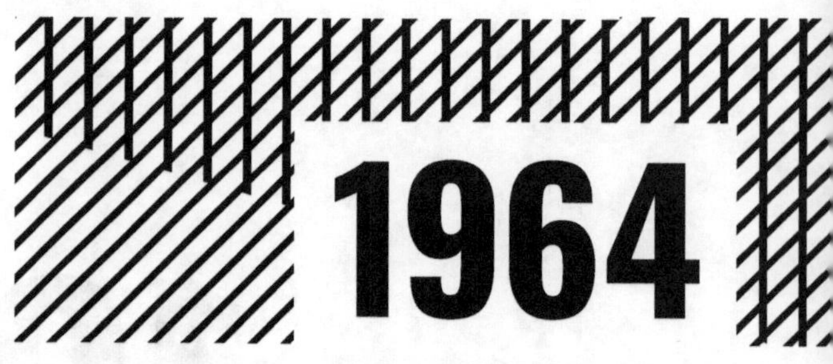

1964

British sociologist, Ruth Glass coins the term **gentrification** in her book *London: Aspects of Change*.

FLUXUS

1962-1978

Integrated life into art through the use of **found events, sounds, and materials**, thereby bringing about social and economic change in the art world.

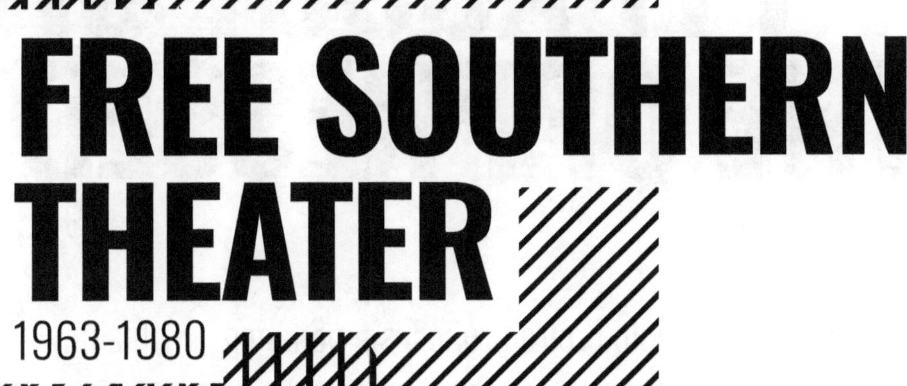

FREE SOUTHERN THEATER

1963-1980

Sought to introduce free theater to the South, both as a **voice for social protest**, and to emphasize **positive aspects of African-American culture.**

EL TEATRO CAMPESINO
1965–present

A theatrical troupe founded as the **cultural arm of the United Farm Workers** with the "full support of Cesar Chavez." The original actors were all farmworkers, and **El Teatro Campesino** enacted events inspired by the lives of their audience.

PEDAGOGY OF THE OPPRESSED
1968

Paulo Freire proposes a pedagogy with a new relationship between **teacher, student, and society**.

CREDITS:
1 > Susan Leibovitz Steinman, "Directional Signs: A Compendium of Artists' Works" in Suzanne Lacy's **Mapping the Terrain: New Genre Public Art** (Bay Press, 1995)
2 > https://feministactivism.com
3 > http://www.tate.org.uk/
4 > Cartiere, Cameron and Martin Zebracki. **The Everyday Practice of Public Art**. Routledge, 2016.

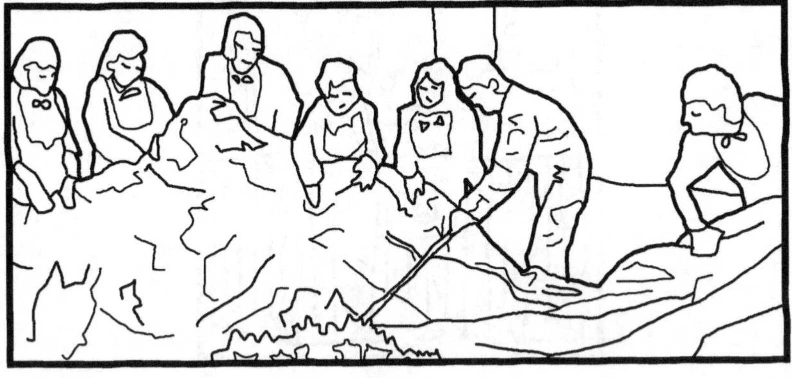

Allison Knowles

Make a Salad

originally presented 1962

Knowles prepares a massive salad, chopping ingredients to live music, collectively tossing the salad, and then serving it to the audience. The work is an early example of a Fluxus event score.

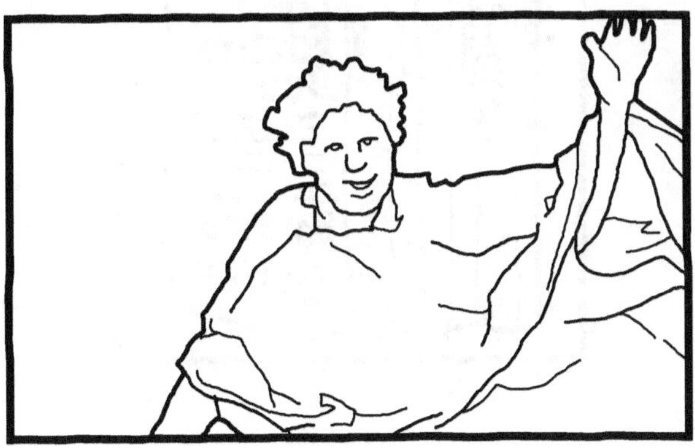

Helio Oiticica

Parangolés

mid-1960s

These were habitable paintings designed to be worn while dancing to the rhythm of samba. Oiticica was frustrated by the limitations of painting, which drove him to find ways to move away from the gallery walls and out into 3-dimensional space.

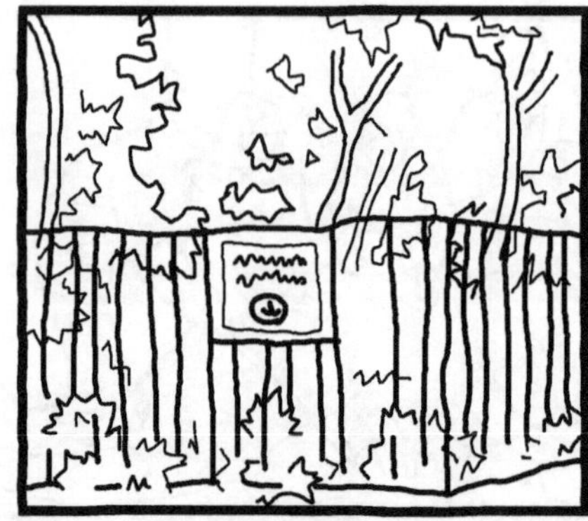

Alan Sonfist

Time Landscape of New York City
1965–continuing

This is the first site-specific public artwork to be maintained permanently by the city's public parks system. Previously it was an abandoned site, and now the soil has been restored and historically accurate native woodlands have been planted. It required ten years of planning and collaboration.

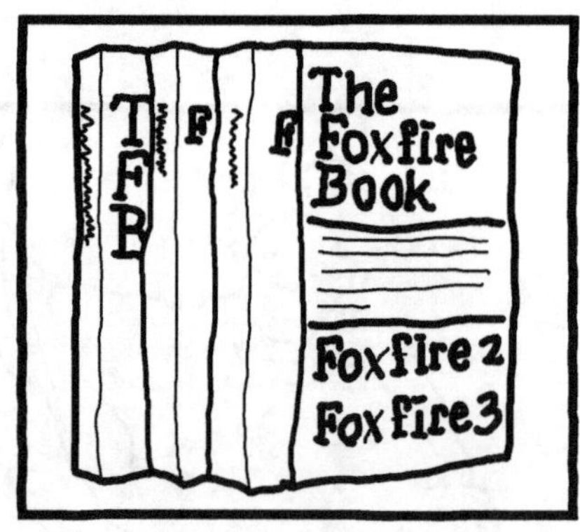

Collaborative Project

The Foxfire Magazine
1967–ongoing

Today, students in the Foxfire classroom at Rabun County High School produce two double-issues each school year, focusing on the stories and talents of people in the surrounding communities and beyond, and on living cultural traditions and Appalachian heritage.

https://www.foxfire.org/about-foxfire/

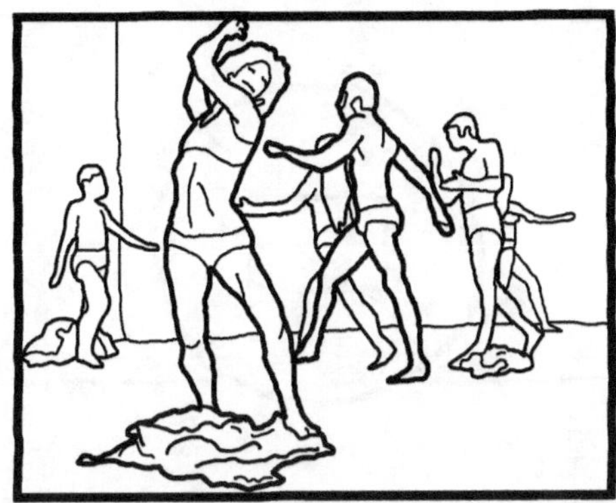

Anna Halprin

Ceremony of Us

1969

After the Watts riots in Los Angeles in 1965, Halprin taught for a year at Studio Watts, where this work was collectively created by local young black people and visiting young white people from the San Francisco-based Dancers' Workshop. The audience for the work had to choose entering a door for black or white people, and at the end of the performance, the audience collectively and spontaneously responded by forming a united procession and dancing together.

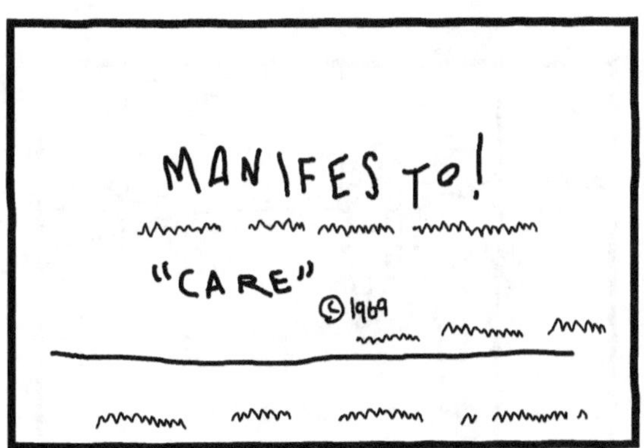

Mierle Laderman Ukeles

Maintenance Art-Proposal for an Exhibition

1969

Laderman Ukeles wrote this manifesto to challenge the domestic role of women and proclaimed herself a "maintenance artist".

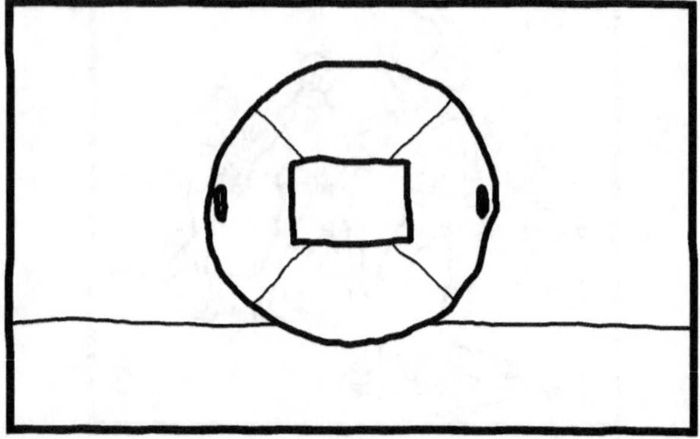

Mary Miss

Portable Window

1968

Miss' work crosses boundaries between landscape architecture, architecture, and urban design. Her vision favors site-specificity and human perception over traditional concerns of the public monument.

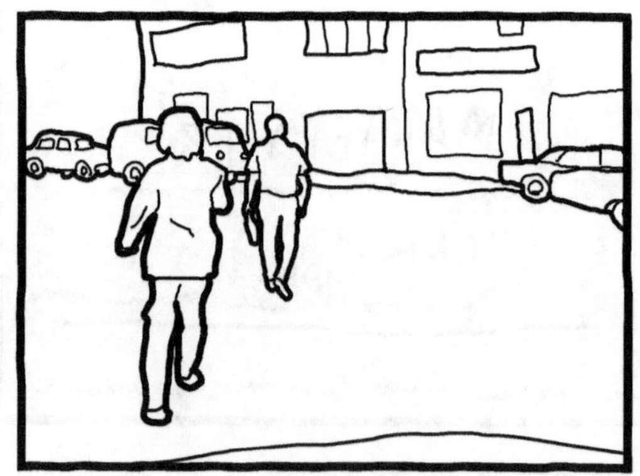

Vito Acconci

Following Piece

1969

The artist selected passersby at random on the streets in New York City and followed them for as long as he was able, questioning ideas of agency and participation.

Some SOCIAL PRACTICE HISTORY

1970s

The history of social practice includes elements of art, social justice, theatre, performance, music, politics, and more. It includes many artists, events, and projects not mentioned here. Here are some **key events around the 1970s...**

PUNK ROCK & DIY

mid-1970s–1980s

Rejected association with the **mainstream**.

BLACK ARTS MOVEMENT
1965-1975

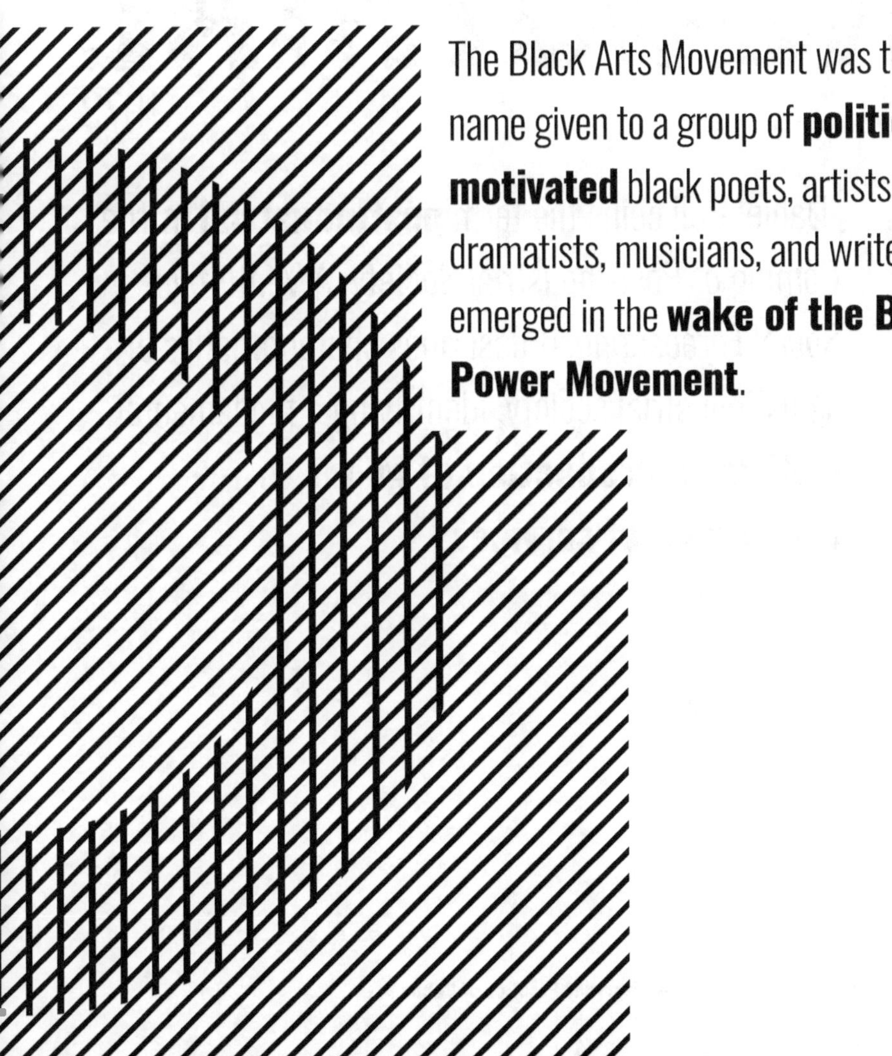

The Black Arts Movement was the name given to a group of **politically motivated** black poets, artists, dramatists, musicians, and writers who emerged in the **wake of the Black Power Movement**.

POST INDUSTRIAL

1973

"Daniel Bell coins the term **postindustrial** in *The Coming of Post-Industrial Society: A Venture in Social Forecasting*. It describes characteristics of a postindustrial society, identifying a fundamental **shift from production of goods to production of services**."

CREDITS:
1 > Cameron Cartiere and Martin Zebracki, **The Everyday Practice of Public Art**
2 > http://www.blackpast.org/

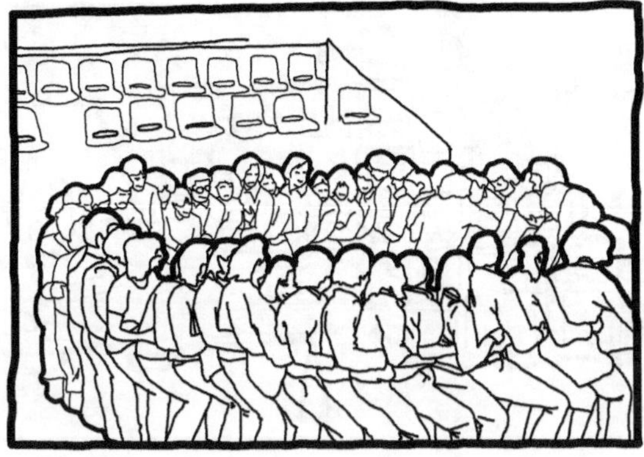

Augusto Boal

The Theatre of the Oppressed
1971

This approach to theatre-making was led by the Brazilian director and political activist Augusto Boal as a form of popular theater, of, by, and for people struggling for liberation.

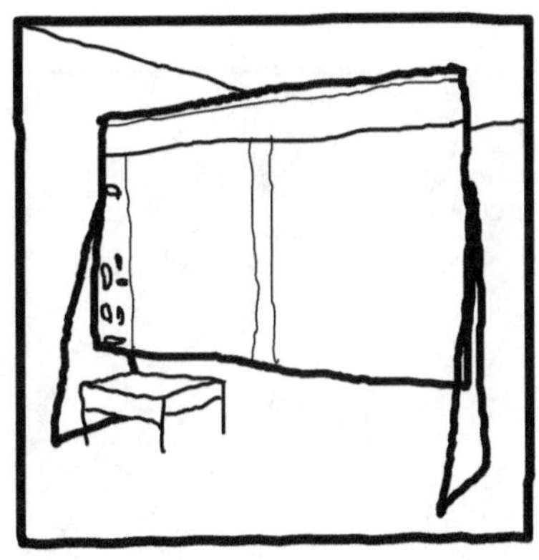

Stephan Willets

West London Social Resources Project
1972-1973

During this time Willets "creates participatory artworks for tower blocks in the UK, Finland, Germany, and Holland, and developed 'modes of resistance and critical conciseness' with residents to critique bureaucratic and civil engineering plans."

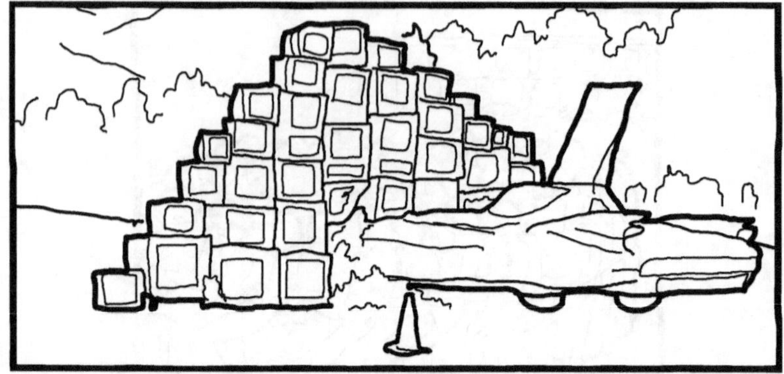

Ant Farm

Media Burn

1975

A widely broadcast performance in front of 400 people featuring a reconfigured Cadillac driving 55 miles per hour through a wall of 50 burning television sets to critique of mass media monopolies.

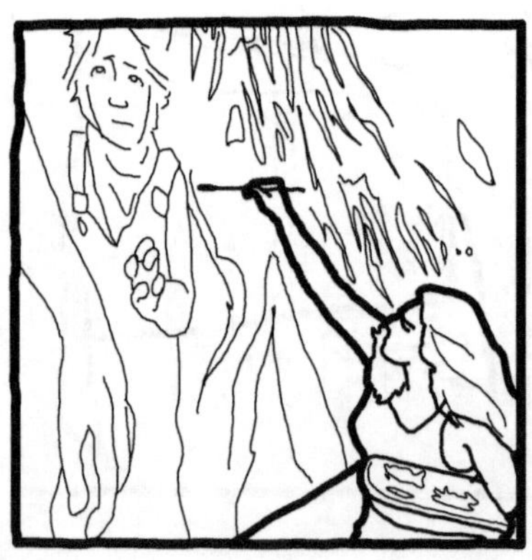

Judith F. Baca

The Great Wall of Los Angeles

1976-ongoing

This ongoing mural project located in a flood control channel in the San Fernando Valley has been painted by hundreds of teenagers who were hired, taught, and directed by Baca. It aims at political activism and education through its subject matter pulled from prehistory through the 1950s.

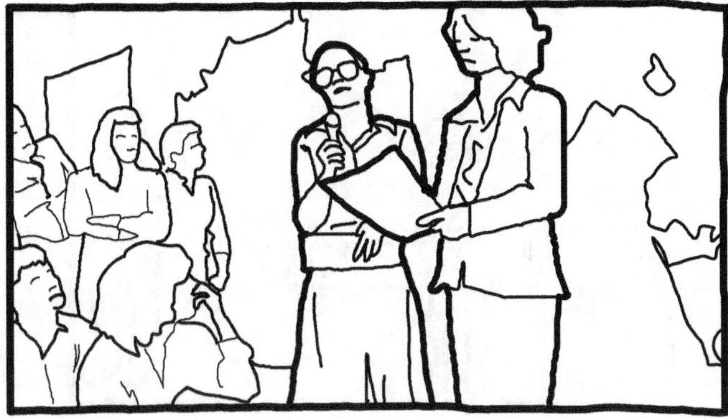

Suzanne Lacy

Three Weeks in May

1977

This project illuminated reported rapes in Los Angeles during a three-week performance in May, 1977. Each day Lacy picked up the previous day's police reports and stamped them on a large public map. Organizations also held various activities for women on violence prevention at sites of resistance around the city.

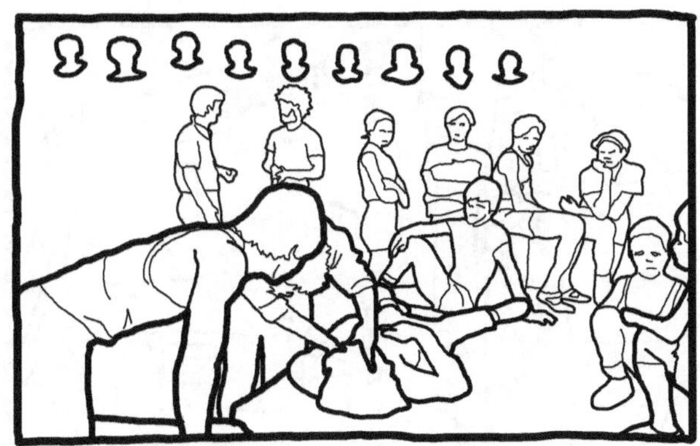

John Ahearn & Rigoberto Torres

South Bronx Hall of Fame

1979

The artists staged public castings of neighborhood residents. The act of being cast became a sign of individual bravado and united the community. The final exhibition took on the sense of an enormous block party.

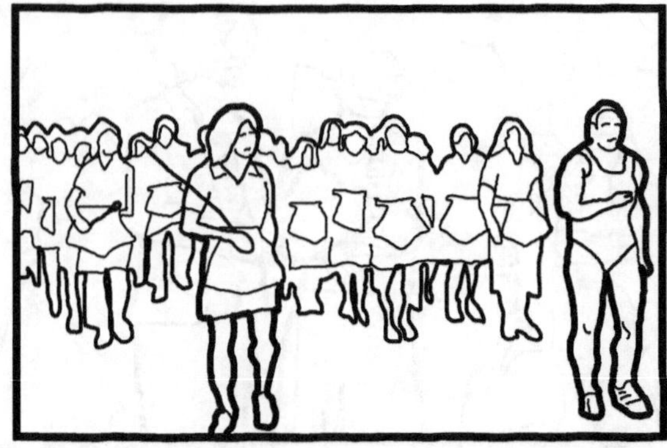

Jerri Allyn, Leslie Belt, and Chutney Gunderson

The All City Waitress Marching Band

1979

Thirty-five Los Angeles waitresses marched and sang to the accompaniment of a pot, pan, and kitchen utensil band publicly displaying unity and voicing empathy for working women.

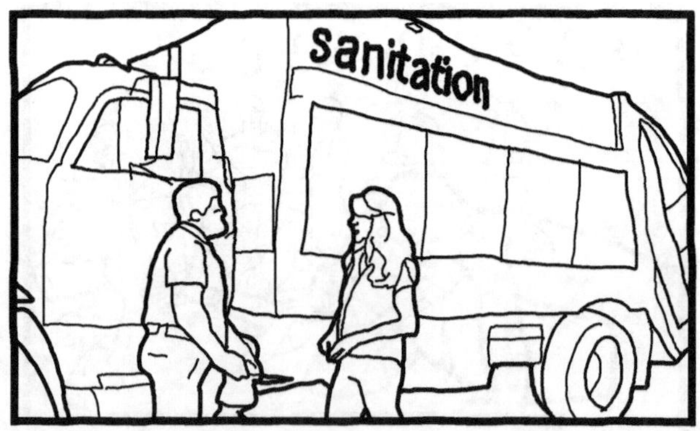

Mierle Laderman Ukeles

Touch Sanitation Performance

1979–1980

The artist spent a year visiting all of the NYC sanitation department's districts to shake hands with all 8,500 workers that would accept the gesture.

Some SOCIAL PRACTICE HISTORY

1980s

The history of social practice includes elements of art, social justice, theatre, performance, music, politics, and more. It includes many artists, events, and projects not mentioned here. Here are some **key events around the 1980s...**

THE SOCIAL LIFE OF SMALL URBAN SPACES

1980

The book (by William H. White) presents Whyte's seminal research on the **Street Life Project** and work with the **New York City Planning Commission**. Whyte critically reflects on his pioneering studies of **pedestrian behavior and city dynamics**.

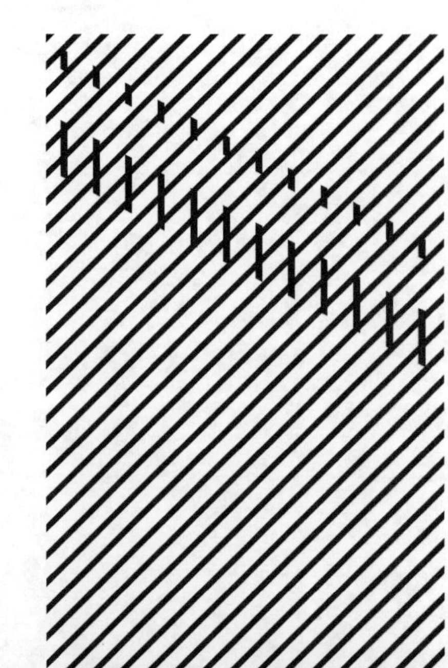

THE CULTURE AND RESISTANCE FESTIVAL

1982

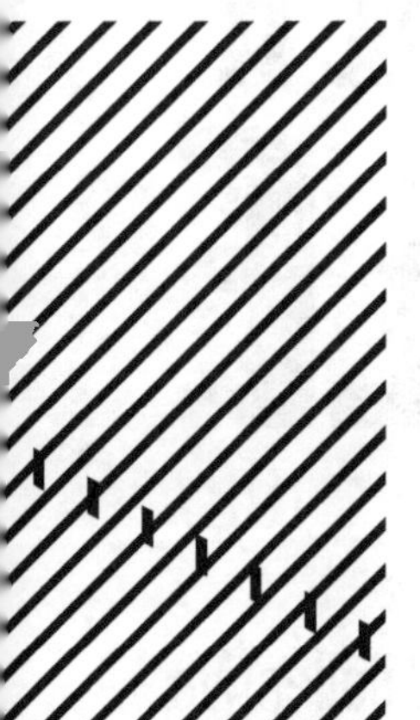

Held in Garobone Botswana, this festival was organised by **Medu Arts Ensemble**, a group of South African **exiled artists, writers, musicians, designers, and theatre practitioners**.

THE PRACTICE OF EVERYDAY LIFE

1984

By Michel de Certeau — this examines the ways in which people **individualise mass culture**; altering things from utilitarian objects to street plans to rituals, laws, and language, in order to make them their own.

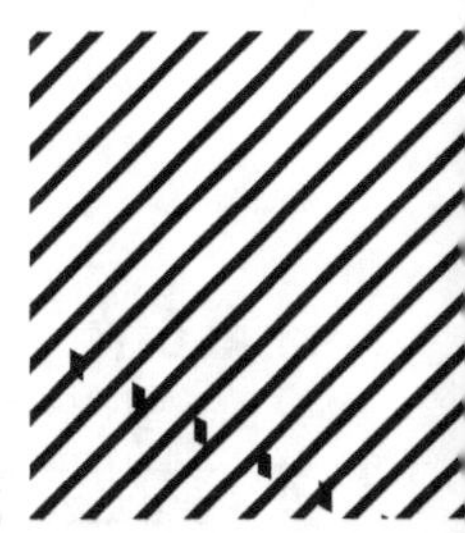

CRITICAL ART ENSEMBLE

1987

The formation of Critical Art Ensemble, an artist collective whose work **explores** and **models** the possibilities for **resistant activity within capitalist democracies** in various **public contexts**.

CREDITS:
1 > Cameron Cartiere and Martin Zebracki, **The Everyday Practice of Public Art**
2 > http://www.theartstory.org/
3 > www.greenparty.org

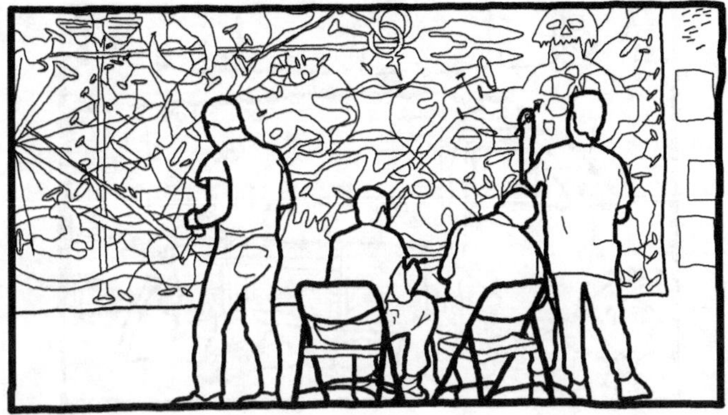

Tim Rollins, Kids of Survival

Rollins and K.O.S.

1981, South Bronx, New York

This began as a project initiated by Rollins to integrate art practice into an after-school literacy program. Rollins shares authorship of the resulting artworks with the Kids of Survival. The original students coined the name K.O.S.

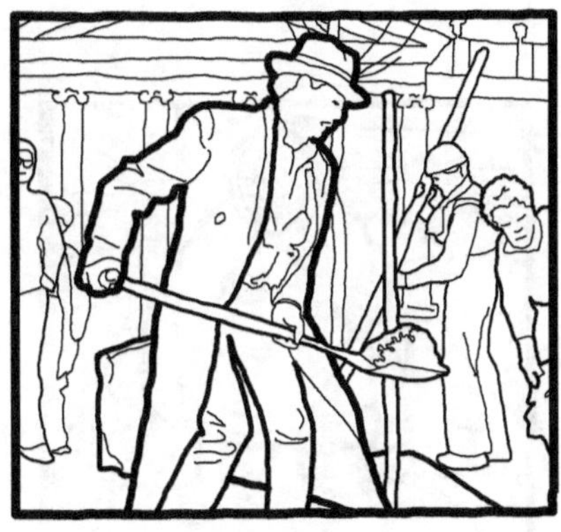

Joseph Beuys

7000 Oaks: City Forestation Instead of City Administration

1982–1987, Kassel, Germany

Beuys planted 7000 trees in Kassel, Germany, over several years (carried out with the assistance of volunteers). Each oak is accompanied by a stone of basalt. This is an example of what Beuys called Social Sculpture; a mode of working that treated audience members as equal participants and embraced art's potential to transform society.

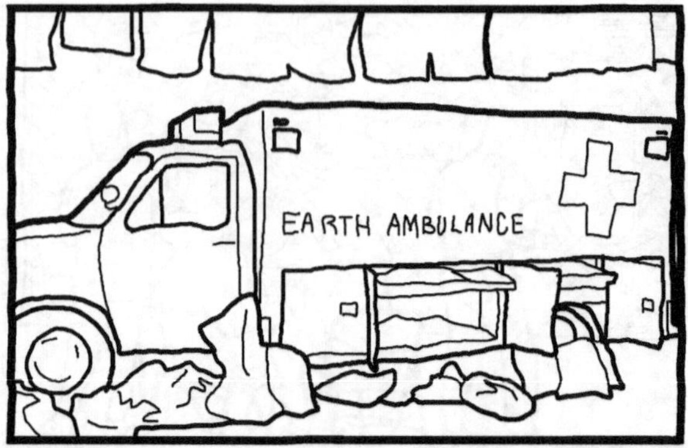

Helene Aylon

The Earth Ambulance

1982–92

Through several iterations, pillowcases of 'endangered earth' were collected/rescued from nuclear weapon sites and displayed to highlight the plight of those who have to flee war zones with only a sack of belongings.

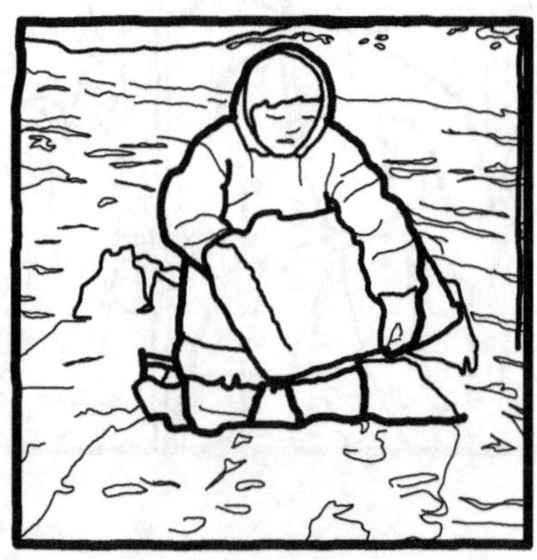

Igloolik Isuma

Productions Nunavut

1983

This project consisted of scripts drawn from interviews with elders, in which they explain traditional parts of their culture—making igloos or sod houses—for younger people to learn from. The young people then act out these scripts on video, and viewers watch them, learning these traditional skills.

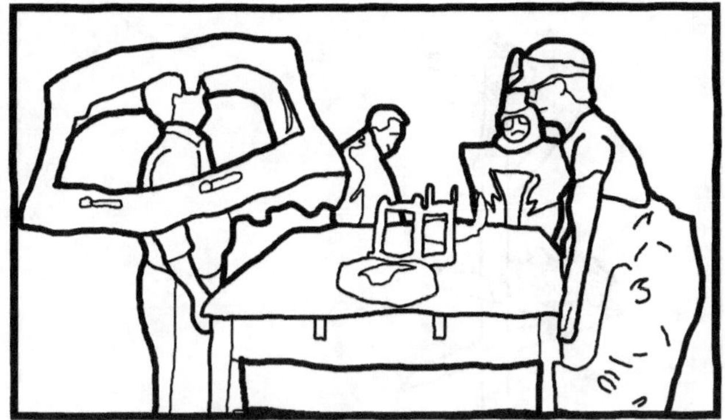

Border Art Workshop / Taller de Arte Fronterizo

End of the Line

1986

A site-specific performance of exchanging food and holding hands at a giant table that bisected the U.S.-Mexican border where it meets the Pacific Ocean.

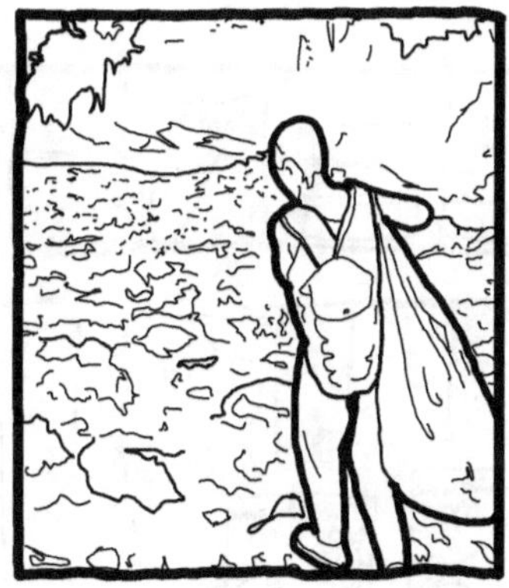

Dominique Mazeaud

The Great Cleansing of the Rio Grande

1987–1994

Once a month on the same date, the artist (and sometimes other participants) would remove trash from the river and its banks. Passersby witnessed the removal and discussed the project with the artist. The artist kept a journal which is often displayed with objects taken from the space when the work is on view.

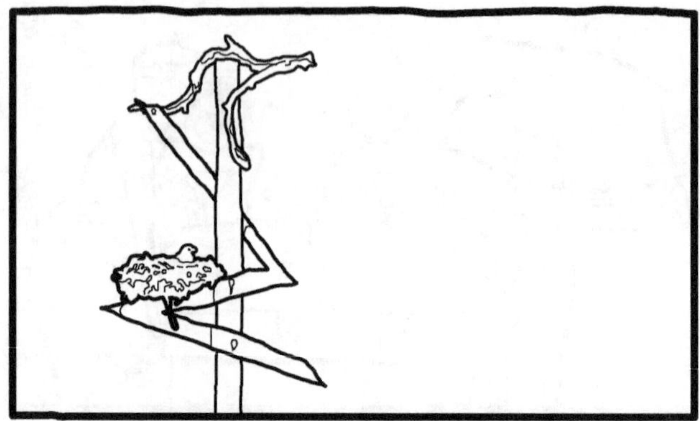

Lynn Hull

Raptor Roosts

1988–1990

Hull installed a series of outdoor sculptures that functioned as roosts and nesting platforms for predatory birds. These were located in areas of Colorado and Wyoming that had been affected by deforestation.

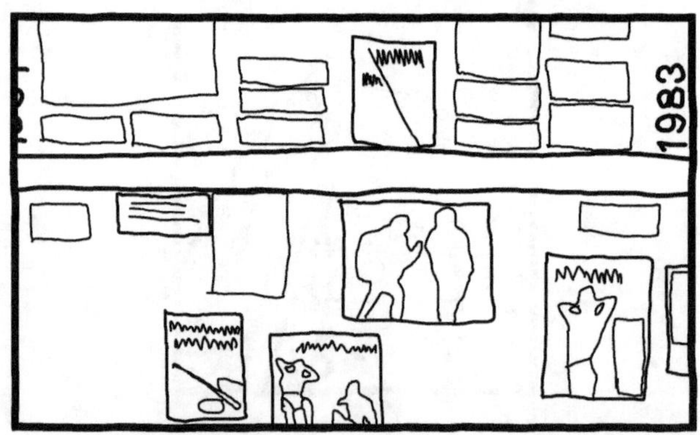

Group Material

AIDS Timeline

1989

Building on the 1984 iteration, this exhibition was curated by Group Material members, showcasing the concept of artist as curator. It diagrammed a decade of AIDS related events via wall text and materials distributed in chronological order.

http://moussemagazine.it/taac4-a/

Some SOCIAL PRACTICE HISTORY

1990s

The history of social practice includes elements of art, social justice, theatre, performance, music, politics, and more. It includes many artists, events, and projects not mentioned here. Here are some **key events around the 1990s...**

NEW GENRE PUBLIC ART

1991

New Genre Public Art is defined in 1991 by Suzanne Lacy as **activist**, often created **outside the institutional structure** which brought the artist into **direct engagement** with the audience, while **addressing social and political issues.**

THE PRODUCTION OF SPACE

1991

Henri Lefebvre's neo-Marxist work examines the **socially constructed** nature of **space**, and complex **social realities** of **everyday life**.

TEACHING TO TRANSGRESS: EDUCATION AS THE PRACTICE OF FREEDOM

1994

Published by bell hooks.

RELATIONAL AESTHETICS

1998

The term Relational Aesthetics is invented by Nicholas Bourriaud and popularized through the publication of a book by the same name. It is art based on, or inspired by, **human relations and their social context**.

CREDITS:
1 > Cameron Cartiere and Martin Zebracki, **The Everyday Practice of Public Art**
2 > Ted Purves and Shane Aslan Selzer, **What We Want is Free**

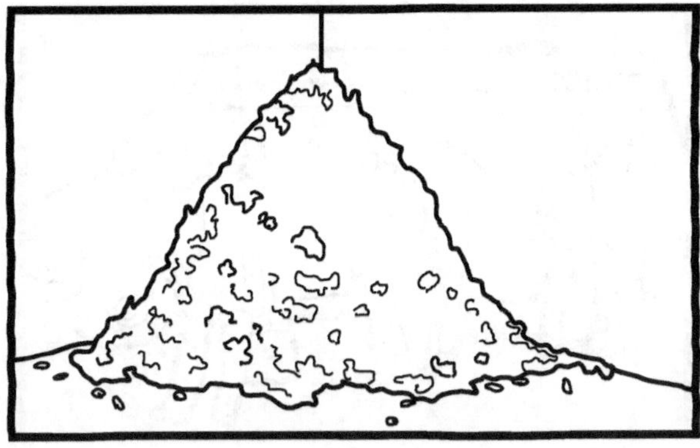

Felix Gonzalez-Torres

Untitled (Portrait of Ross in LA)
1991, endless supply of wrapped candies, ideal weight 175 lbs

As participants take candies from the pile, they slowly disperse the portrait of Ross, Gonzalez-Torres' lover who died of AIDS.

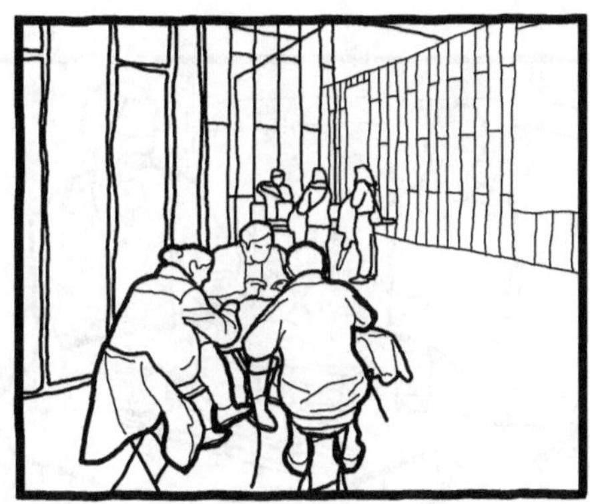

Rirkrit Tiravanija

untitled 1992/1995 (free/still)
1992, 1995

The artist transferred everything from the gallery's back office, including staff, to the gallery itself and cooked curry and rice, serving it to visitors free of charge, exploring the possibility of creating friendly social spaces in places typically reserved for the quiet contemplation of art.

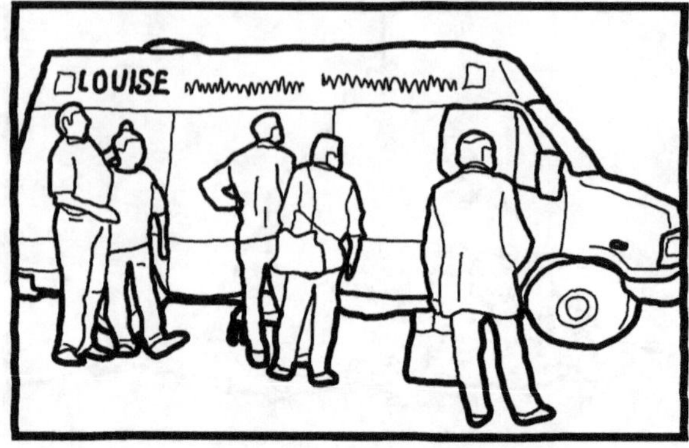

Wochenklausur

Medical Care for Homeless People

1993

Set up a mobile clinic for providing basic medical treatment, which visits places in Vienna frequented by homeless people, providing more than 700 treatments per month.

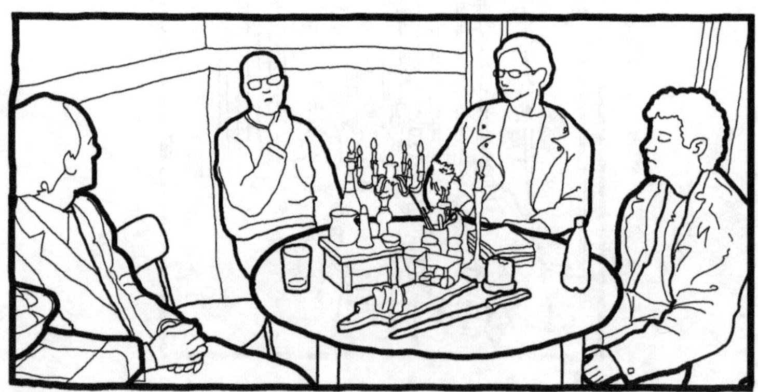

Diana Mars

Any Wednesday

1993-ongoing

This was a regular weekly dinner in Mars' apartment, free of charge and advertised discreetly through word of mouth and handmade calling cards. No one was required to bring food, however many often did.

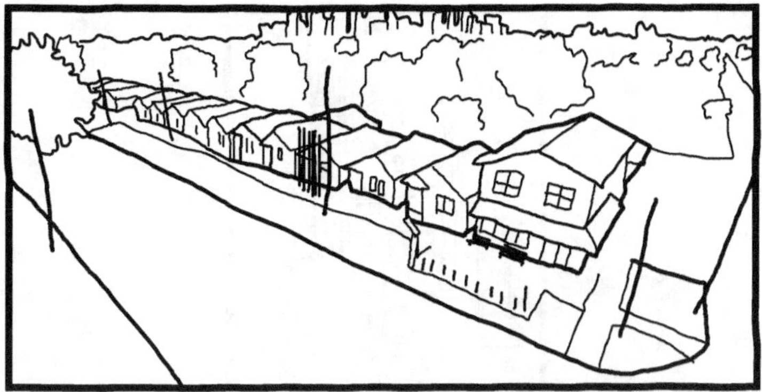

Rick Lowe

Project Row Houses
1993–ongoing, Houston, TX

PRH works to revitalize Houston's Third Ward Using architecture (23 historic shotgun houses), social networks, tax/zoning policy, affordable housing, paint, music, and sculpture.

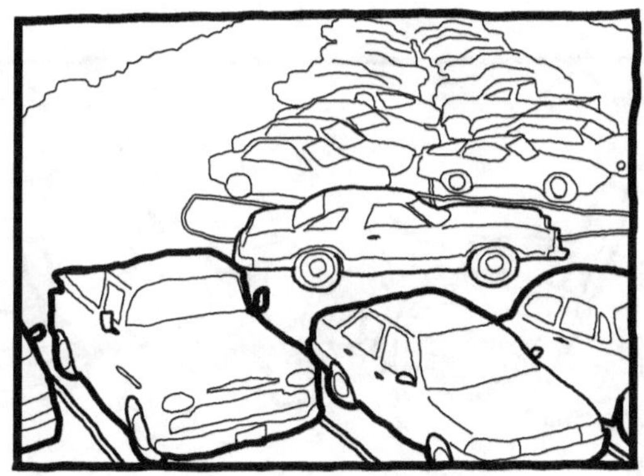

Nina Katchadourian, Steven Matheson, Mark Tribe

CARPARK
1994 — Part of inSITE'94, at Southwestern College, Chula Vista, CA

For one half-day, the artists, with the help of 50 volunteers, sorted all the incoming cars by color into 14 different parking lots at the school. To generate awareness and enthusiasm for the event, they mounted a huge informational campaign.

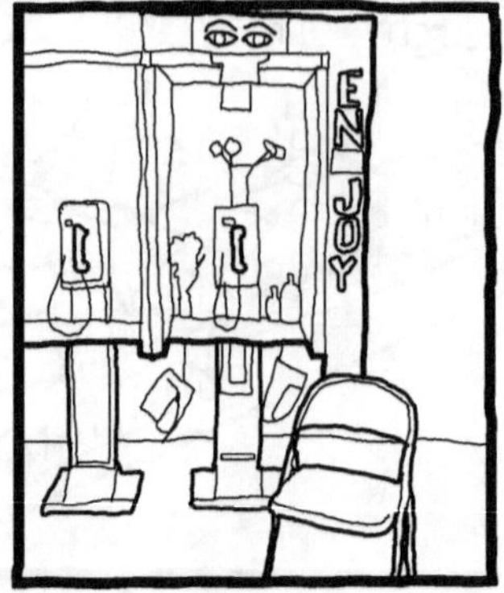

Sophie Calle

Gotham Handbook: Keep Smiling

1994

Author Paul Auster sent Calle *Personal Instructions for SC on How to Improve Life in New York City (Because she asked...)*. Following these instructions, Calle went to New York, and took over a phone booth where she provided a variety of luxuries to users including water, flowers and cigarettes.

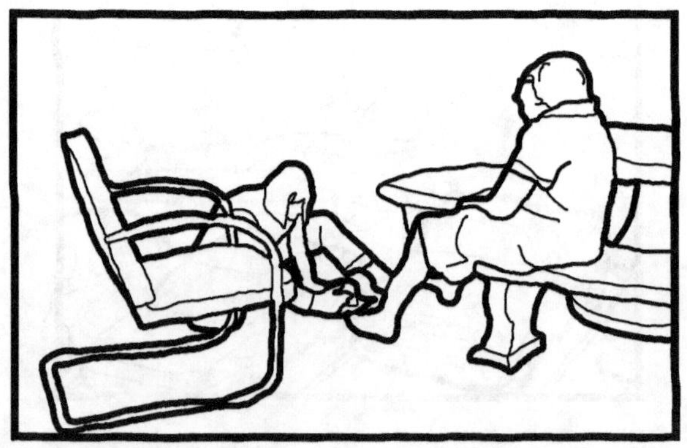

Jackie Brookner

Of Cotton & Earth, (process shot)

1994–98

At 7 locations from the Carolinas to Texas, she spoke with people who farmed/picked cotton by hand in the 1930's and 40's, and sat on the ground sculpting portraits of their feet out of nearby soil.

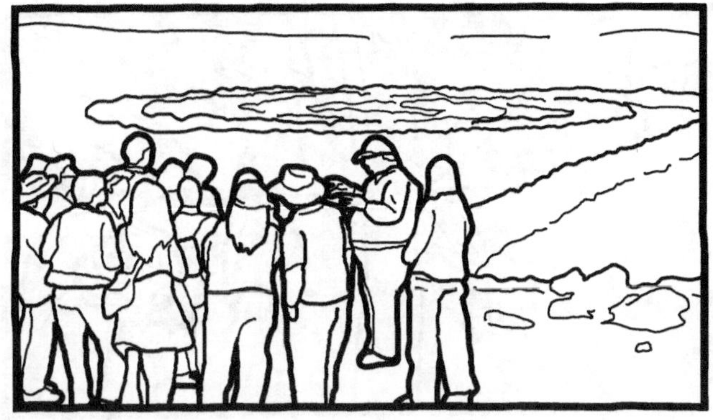

Center for Land Use Interpretation

Tour of The Monuments of the Great American Void

1994–ongoing

Based in Culver City, California, the CLUI explores how land is appropriated and utilized.

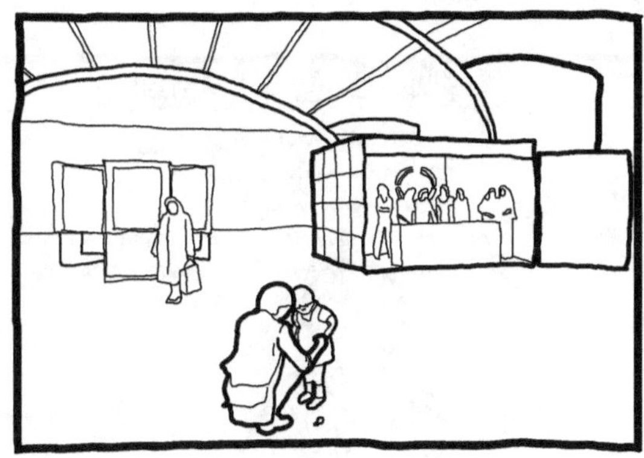

Alicia Framis

Compagnie de Compagnie

1996

Installed in a Utrecht shopping mall that closed at 6pm, this stand contained 13 pairs of identical twins, who Framis considered experts in togetherness. Lonely evening travelers could check out a pair of twins for a short walk determined by the traveler.

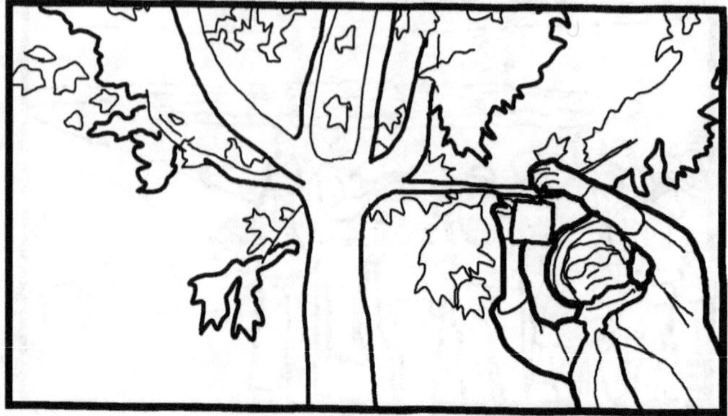

Yoko Ono

Wish Tree

1996

Ono asks participants to write down wishes on cards, and hang them on a tree. The museum staff then gathers the wishes and returns them to Ono, who buries them at the base of her *Imagine Peace Tower* in Reykjavik, Iceland.

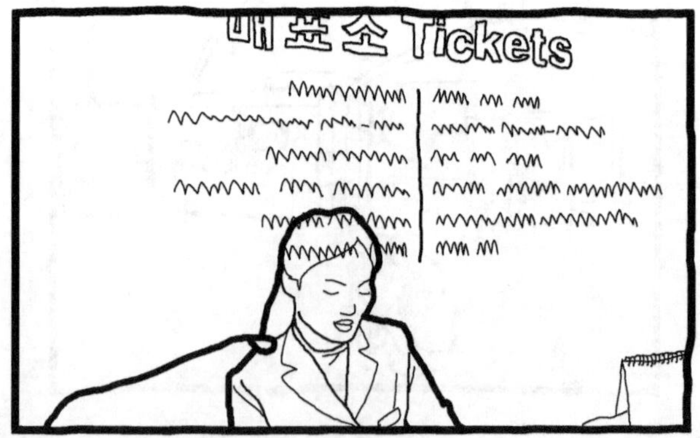

Jens Haaning

Foreigners Free

1997-2001

This work was executed in seven different countries as a part of various group exhibitions. Each time it was on display, anyone that was a foreigner to the country hosting the exhibition was admitted for free.

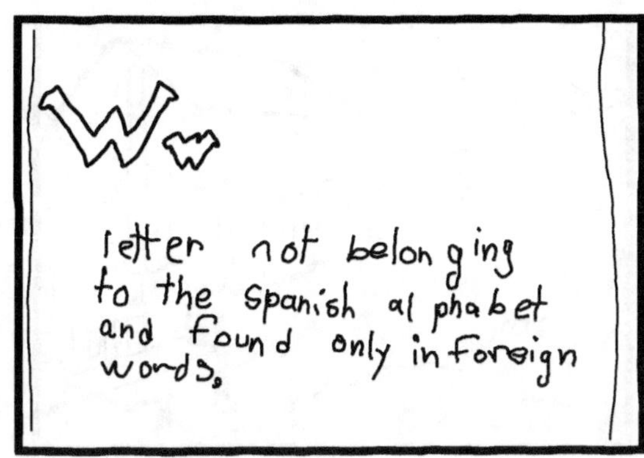

Wendy Ewald

American Alphabets

1997-2005

Inspired by children's alphabet primers, Ewald worked with diverse young people to develop and photograph customized alphabets that illustrated each one's specific way of life. "Taken as a whole, their lists of words amounted to a kind of cultural self-portrait."

http://wendyewald.com/portfolio/american-alphabets/

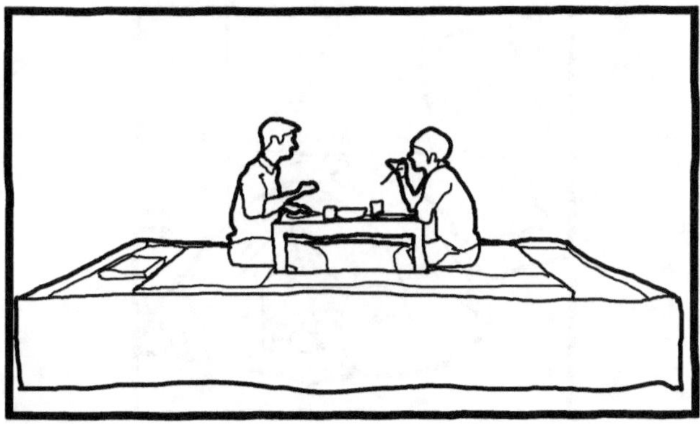

Lee Mingwei

The Dining Project

1997 & 2012

The artist deployed a lottery to select a handful of guests who dine individually with the artist after hours in a museum. Mingwei prepared these meals and recorded audio, which is altered and played at a low volume during museum hours.

http://www.leemingwei.com/projects.php

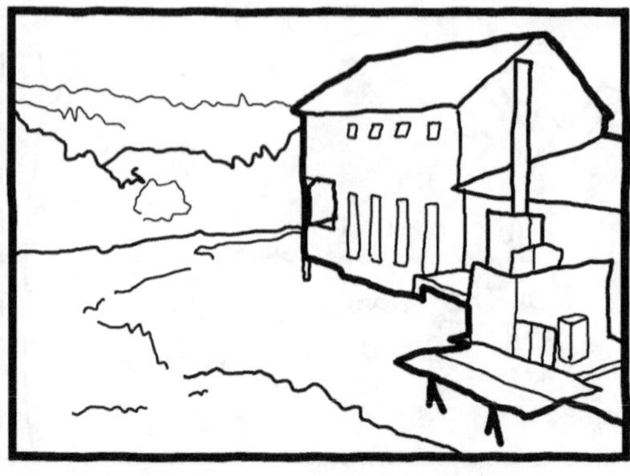

J. Morgan Puett, Mark Dion, Grey Rabbit Puett

Mildred's Lane
1998–ongoing

A 94-acre, wildish site deep in the woods of north-eastern Pennsylvania. A place for social investigations into relations to people and to the environment, systems of labor, forms of dwelling, clothing apparatuses, and inventive domesticating.

http://www.jmorganpuett.com/mildreds-lane

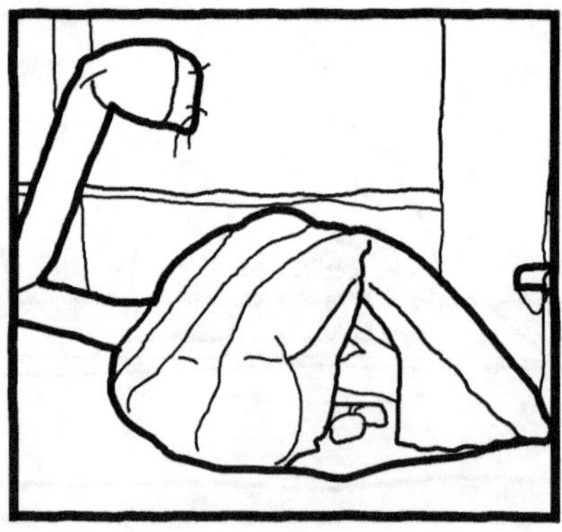

Michael Rakowitz

paraSITE
1998–ongoing

Inflatable shelters designed for homeless people that attach to the exterior vents of a building's Heating, Ventilation, and Air Conditioning (HVAC) system. The warm air leaving the building inflates and heats the structure. Built and distributed to over 30 homeless people in Boston and Cambridge, MA and New York City.

http://www.michaelrakowitz.com/parasite

Some SOCIAL PRACTICE HISTORY

2000s

The history of social practice includes elements of art, social justice, theatre, performance, music, politics, and more. It includes many artists, events, and projects not mentioned here. Here are some **key events around the 2000s...**

CCA & PSU

2005 & 2007

Ted Purves starts first social practice MFA at California College of Art in **2005**, and **Harrell Fletcher** proposes the social practice MFA at Portland State University in **2007**.

OPEN ENGAGEMENT

2007-2018

Open Engagement is an annual **artist-led conference** dedicated to expanding the dialogue around and **creating a site of care** for the field of **socially engaged art**. The conference highlights the work of transdisciplinary artists, activists, students, scholars, community members, and organizations **working within** the complex **social issues** and **struggles of our time**.

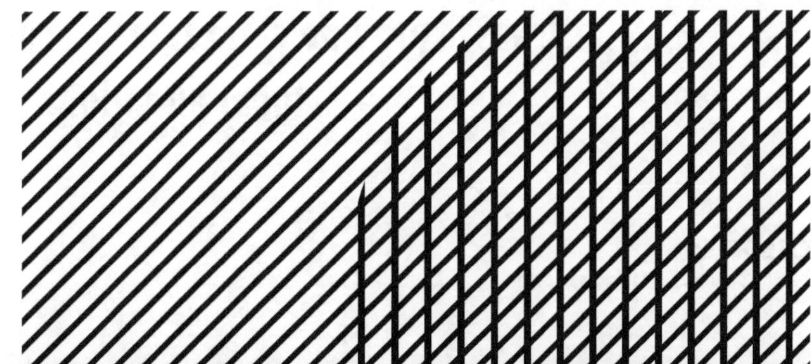

CREATIVE TIME SUMMIT

2009

Creative Time Summit began in 2009, and continues as an **annual conference** for people working at the **intersection of art** and **politics**. It strives to **provide strategies** for social change in **local and global contexts**.

CREDITS:
1 > Nato Thompson, **Living as Form**

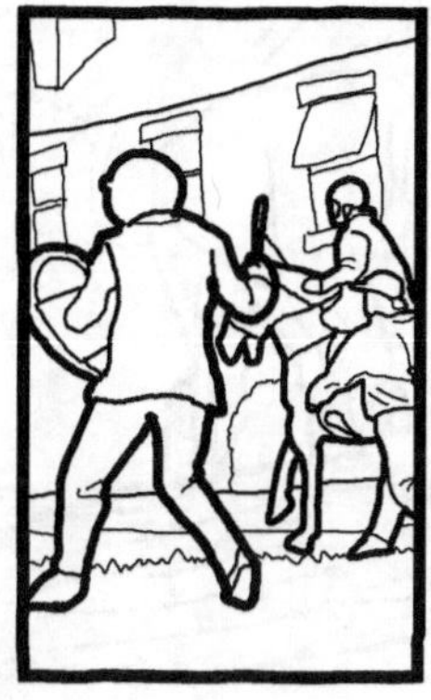

Jeremy Deller

The Battle of Orgreave

2001

This project was a re-enactment of a 1984 miners' strike, in which striking miners were chased up a hill and pursued through a village. The artist asked 800 re-enactors and 200 veterans of the original event to participate in the staging of this battle, which occurred within the living memory of both the veterans and many of the viewers.

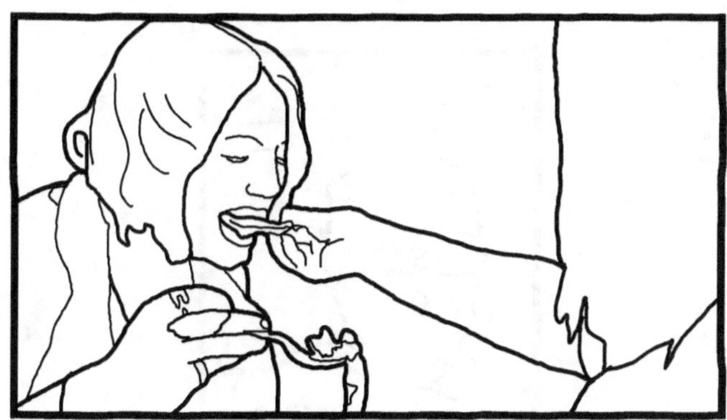

Mella Jaarsma

I Eat You Eat Me

2001–2012

This interactive piece asks participants sit close to one another wearing a leather bib joined to the table that hovers between them. They then order food for the person in front of them and subsequently to feed each other.

http://mellajaarsma.com/project/i-eat-you-eat-me/

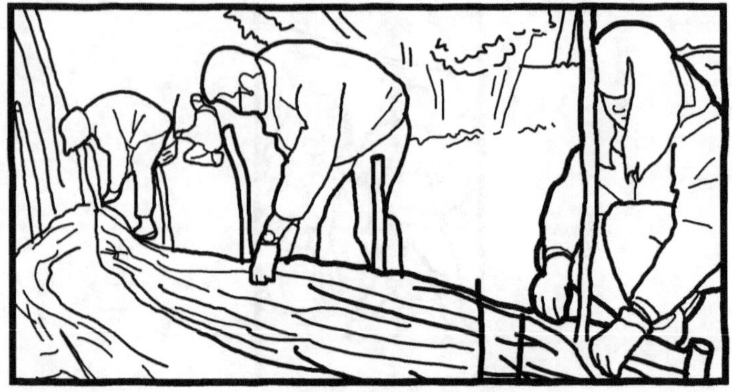

Oliver Kellhammer

Means of Production

2002–ongoing

This project consists of community-scale ecoforestry in a low-income, inner city neighborhood of Vancouver, and frames questions about the loss of the notion of the 'commons' in the North American landscape.

`http://oliverk.org/?q=node/171`

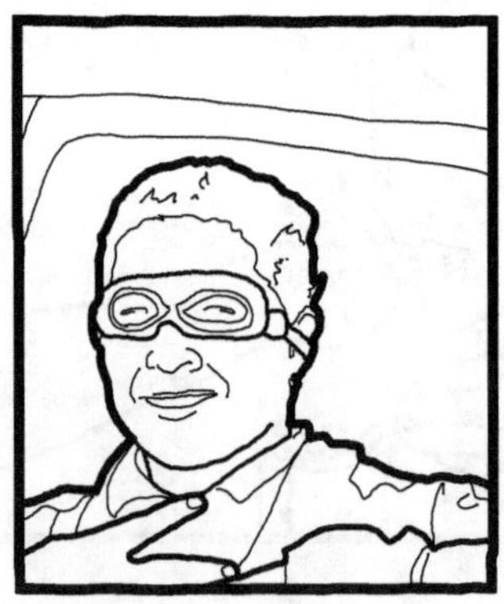

It Can Change

Clothing Project

2003

This project involves artists interested in producing wearable artworks. The pieces are given to the first person that expresses interest in wearing them, and they are instructed to pass them on to the next interested person, and so on.

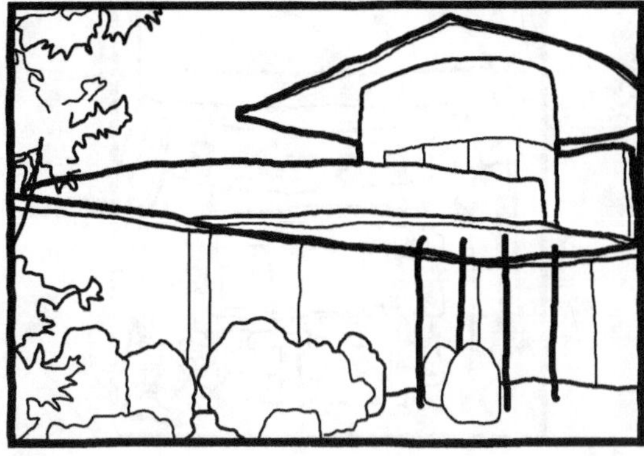

Josep-Maria Martín

Prototype of Space to Deal with Hospital Emotions

2003–05

An architectural structure expressing the idea of, and need for, transition related to hospital stays.

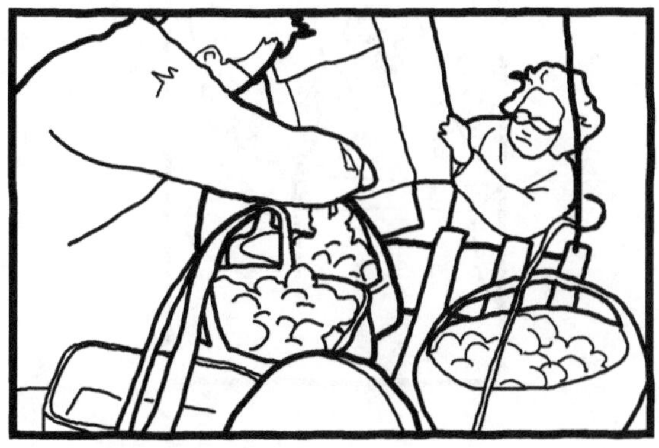

Fieldfaring (Susanne Cockrell & Ted Purves)

Temescal Amity Works

2004–07

This project consisted of *The Reading Room*, a meeting space for public events and project contextualization, and *The Big Back Yard*, a collection of citrus trees and a cart to redistribute the fruit, in various forms, to the community.

https://fieldfaring.wordpress.com/temescal-amity-works/

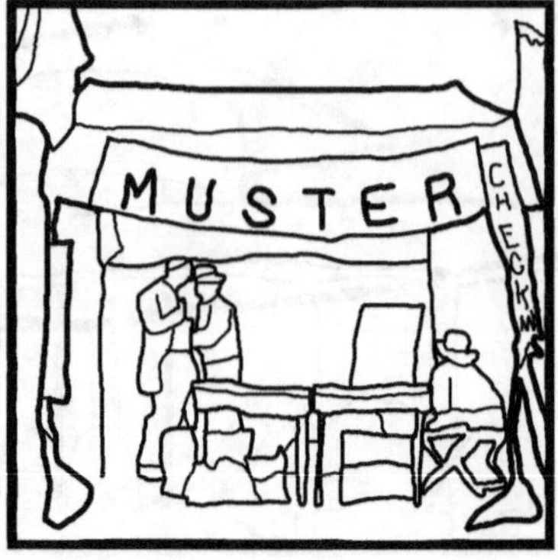

Allison Smith

The Muster

2005

This was an open-air public event during which Smith appointed herself Mustering Officer and asked, "What are you fighting for?" 70+ volunteers created a temporary "militia" and designed their own uniforms and campsites expressing their causes, which ranged from art history, technology, craft, and gender politics, to gay rights, democracy and sociology.

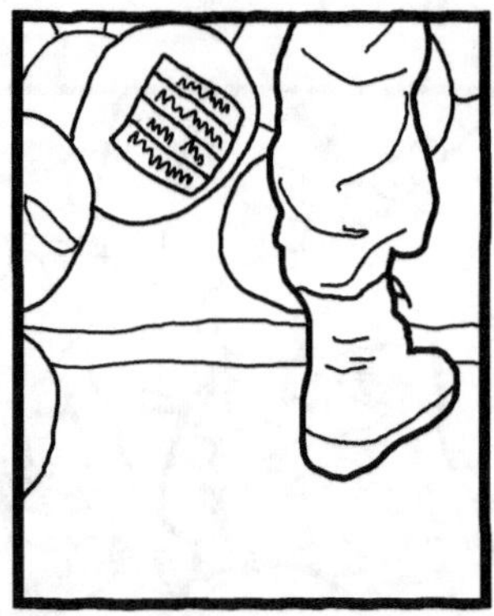

Ultra-red

Public Citizen

2005

After a series of discussions with groups in Germany about issues of community, residency, citizenship and migration, audio tracks were published featuring conversation excerpts ,and sounds recorded during a protest of the German Government's contract with Lufthansa Airlines for the detention and deportation of refugees.

http://www.ultrared.org/ps07a.html

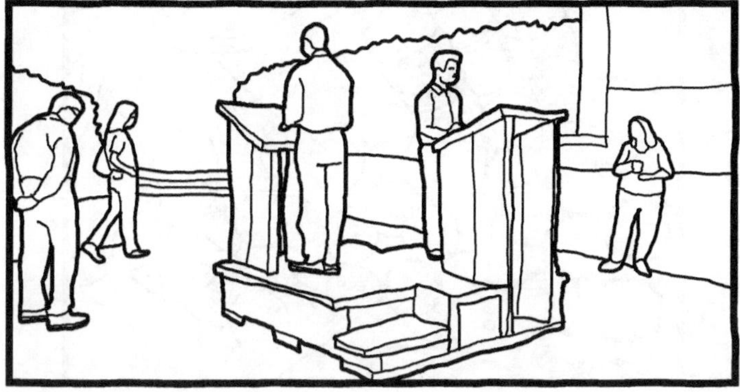

Dan Peterman

Love Podium

2006

This was a functional platform for spoken performances at deCordova Sculpture Park and Museum. Speakers activated the work by simultaneously reading texts that represent opposing views on a single topic.

https://decordova.org/art/exhibition/platform-10-dan-peterman

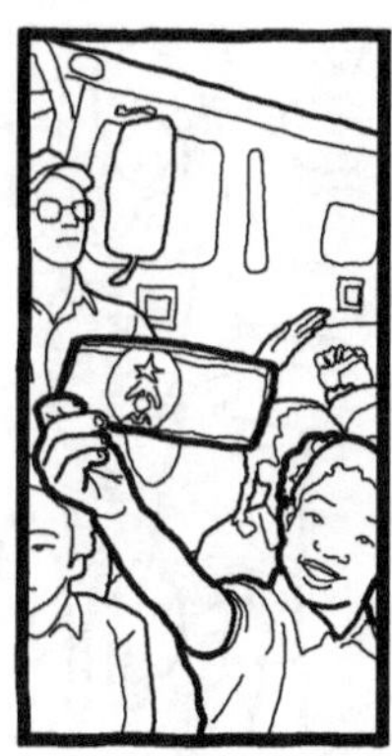

Mel Chin

Operation Paydirt / Fundred Dollar Bill Project

2006-ongoing

This project raises awareness of lead-poisoning by recruiting children to draw 'Fundred' dollar bills, which will be delivered to congress in order to garner support for lead-poisoning solutions.

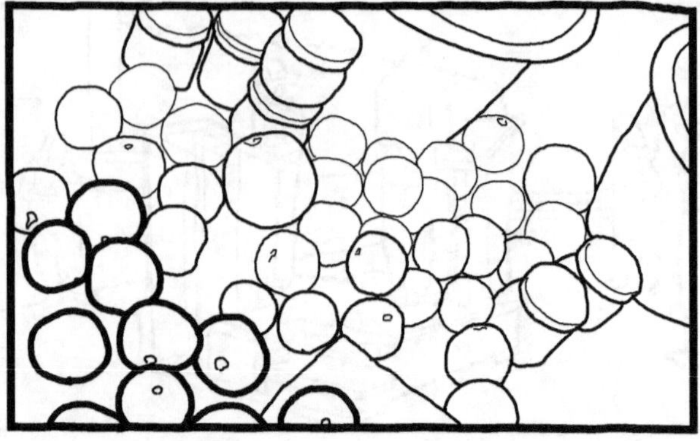

Fallen Fruit

Public Fruit Jam
2006-ongoing

This collective works to create maps of fruit trees growing on or over public spaces. Participants are then invited to bring fruit collected from these trees to gatherings at museums or galleries where they work in groups to create jam.

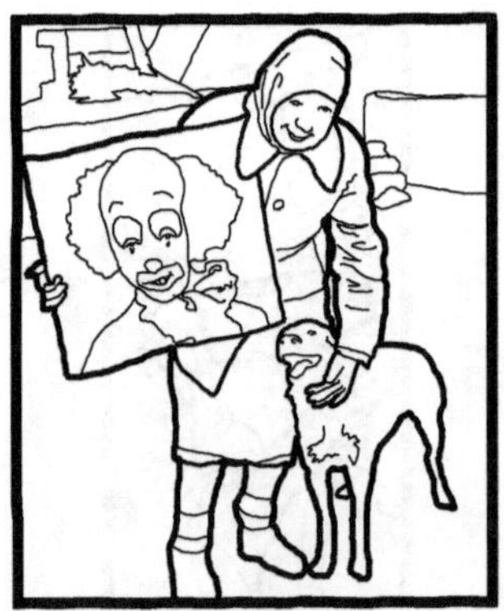

SOSka Group

Barter
2007

This Ukrainian artist collective brought prints of famous artworks by artists such as Cindy Sherman, Chuck Close, and Warhol, to a small village and attempted to trade the prints for local goods. They yielded potatoes, a chick, pickles, eggs, and more. They also photographed the prints with the farmers and their placement in the farmers' homes.

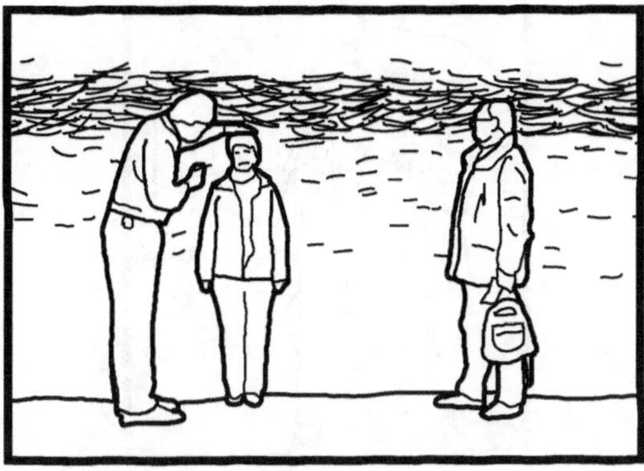

Roman Ondák

Measuring the Universe

2007

Museum guards used black pens to record, on the museum wall, the names and heights of visitors, and the date of their visit, referencing the common childhood experience of standing next to a door-frame and having an adult record the increase in your height.

```
https://www.studiointernational.com/index.php/roman-ondak-
the-source-of-art-is-in-the-life-of-a-people-south-london-
gallery
```

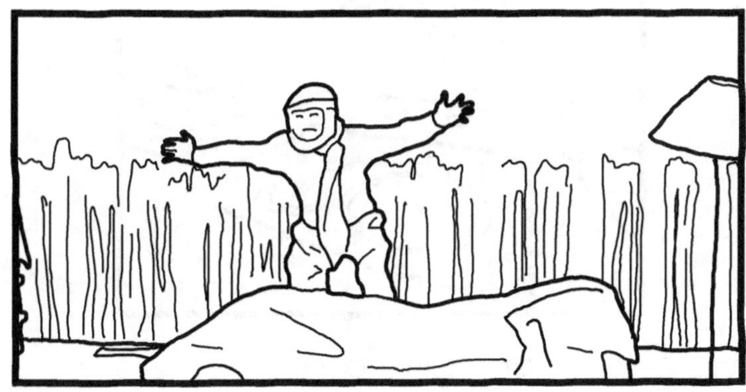

Wafaa Bilal

Shoot an Iraqi

2007

The artist spent a month in an interactive performance where people online could control a paint ball gun aimed at his living space.

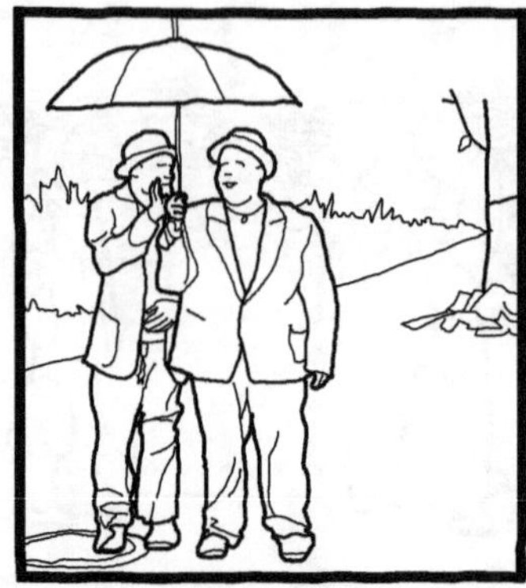

Paul Chan

Waiting for Godot

2007

About a year after Hurricane Katrina hit New Orleans, Chan visited and was struck by "...the cruel and funny things people do while they wait for help, for food, for tomorrow." He decided to work with locals to stage a free outdoor version of Beckett's *Waiting for Godot*, which evolved into a larger series of events and a fundraiser.

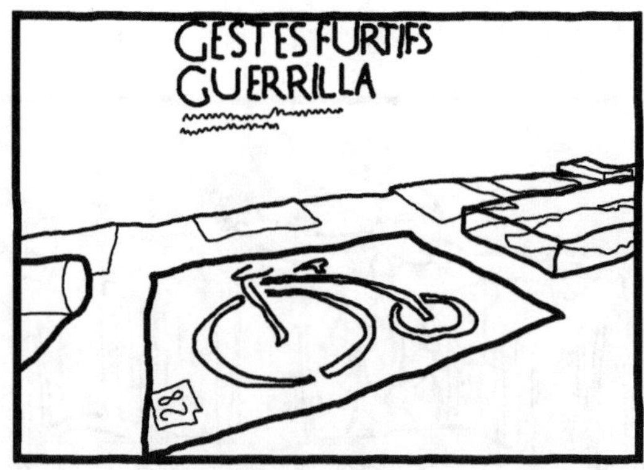

The Canadian Centre for Architecture (CCA)

Actions: What You Can Do With the City

2008–09

An exhibition comprised of 99 specific actions that investigate positive change in cities around the world.

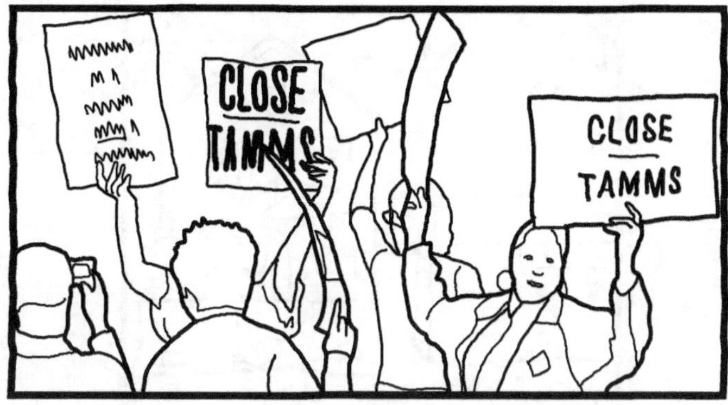

Laurie Jo Reynolds

Tamms Year Ten

2008–2013, Southern Illinois

This project was a partnership with inmates, former inmates, families, lawyers, and concerned citizens. They used artistic actions and interventions to advocate for the closure of a sensory deprivation supermax prison.

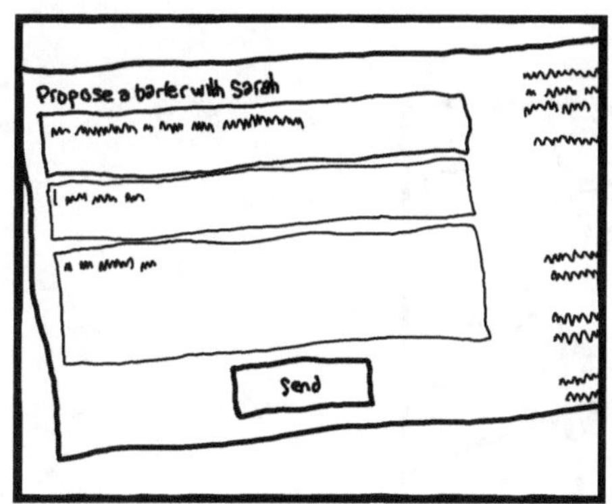

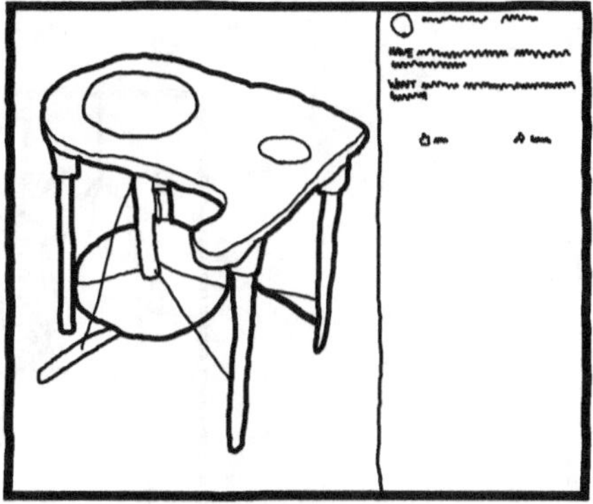

Louise Ma, Rich Watts, Carl Tashian, Jen Abrams, and Caroline Woolard

OurGoods

2008–ongoing

OurGoods is a resource sharing network for the creative community. Its members trade skills, spaces and objects to get their work done without money. They run live events, a Facebook group, and a newsletter.

http://ourgoods.org

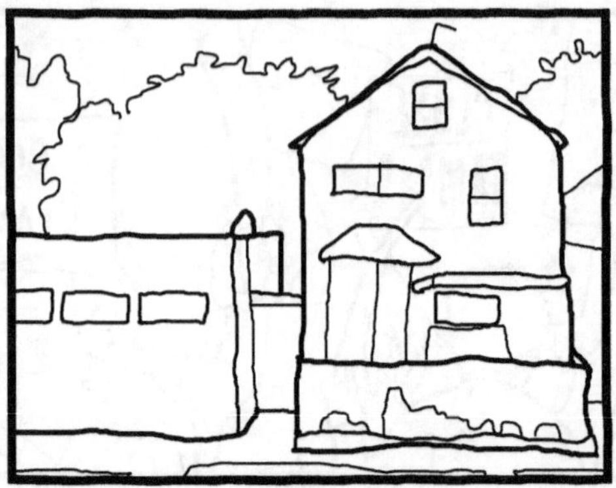

Theaster Gates

Listening House and Archive House
2009-Ongoing

Gates acquired this property for reuse as a gallery, community nexus, and archive for Dr. Wax records, portions of the Johnson Publishing Library, and remaining stock from the now-closed Prairie Avenue Books.

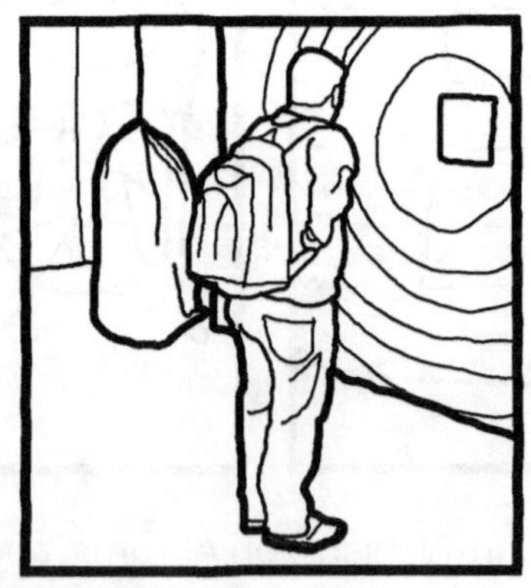

Ashley Hunt and taisha paggett

Par Course A
2009–Ongoing

Organized as a "parcourse" fitness circuit with simple, time-based instructions, engaging the viewer/participant in a minor performance at 11 stations with equipment and instructions.

Some SOCIAL PRACTICE HISTORY

2010s

The history of social practice includes elements of art, social justice, theatre, performance, music, politics, and more. It includes many artists, events, and projects not mentioned here. Here are some **key events around the 2010s...**

LEONORE ANNENBERG PRIZE FOR ART AND SOCIAL CHANGE

2009–2014

Awarded to individuals whose work focused on productive social change.

OCCUPY WALL STREET

2011

A protest **against social** and **economic inequality, greed, corruption** and the **undue influence** of corporations **on government**—particularly **from the financial services sector**.

BLACK LIVES MATTER

2013–present

Beginning as a hashtag after the death of **Trayvon Martin** and the acquittal of his killer in 2013, the Black Lives Matter movement rose to prominence in response to similar events in **Baltimore**, Maryland, and **Ferguson**, Missouri in 2014 and 2015. The group speaks out **against police brutality against black people** and **racial inequality within the US justice system**.

CREDITS:
1 > http://taniabruguera.com/
2 > https://www.conflictkitchen.org/
3 > http://jodywoodart.com/
4 > http://pablohelguera.net/

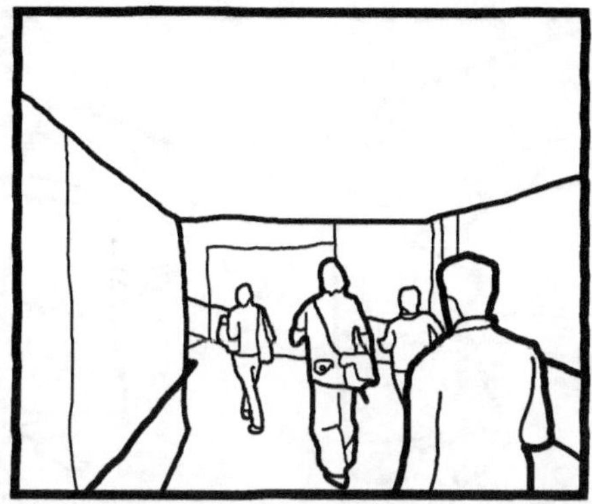

Hui-min Tsen

On the Trail of a Disorderly Future

2010

A series of free, guided tours through the Chicago Pedway—a circuitous and ever-changing route of indoor passageways throughout downtown. The tours speculate on various changing Utopic visions that have shaped not only city development, but also American culture.

`http://huimintsen.com/ht/pedway/`

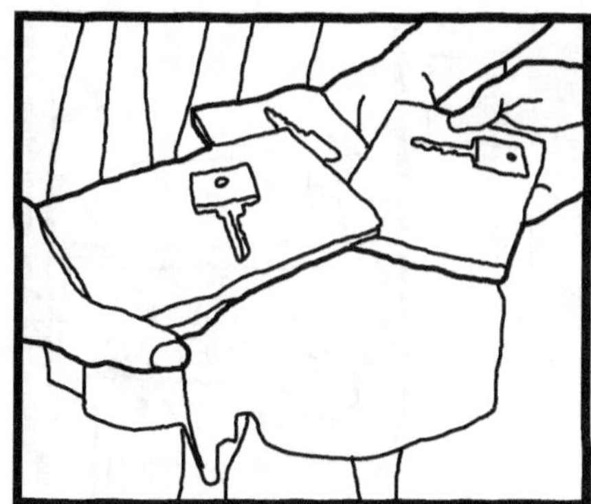

Paul Ramírez Jonas

Key to the City

2010

This project consisted of bestowed the key to New York City to both celebrated and everyday people. The keys unlocked 20+ sites across New York City's boroughs, which encouraged individuals to explore locations such as community gardens, cemeteries, police stations, and museums.

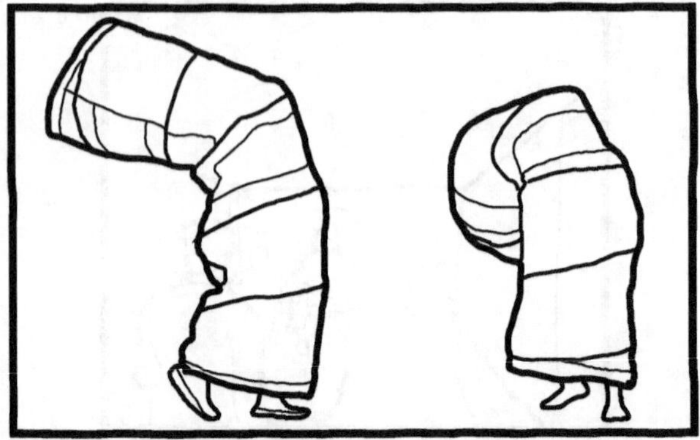

Sarah Peters and Sarah Schultz

Walker Art Center: Open Field

2010–12

This was a three-year, summer-long participatory project of the Walker Art Center that adopts the commons as a philosophical and programmatic framework to imagine a new kind of public gathering space on a four-acre lawn adjacent to the building.

https://walkerart.org/magazine/open-field-book-intro-sarah-schultz-pete

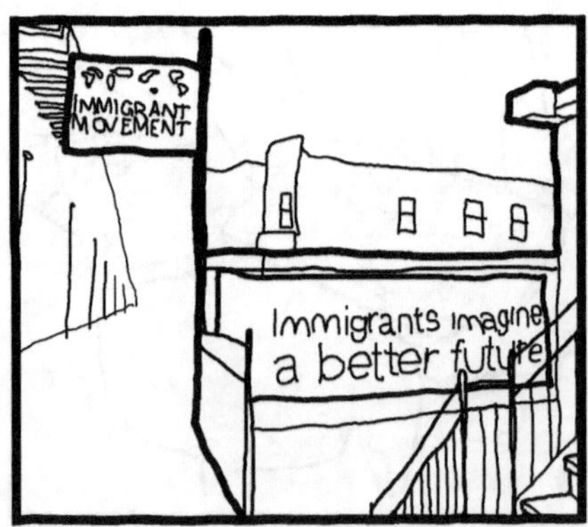

Tania Bruguera

Immigrant Movement International

2010-15

This was a long-term art project in the form of an artist initiated socio-political movement. Bruguera spent a year operating a flexible community space in the multinational and transnational neighborhood of Corona, Queens, which served as the movement's headquarters.

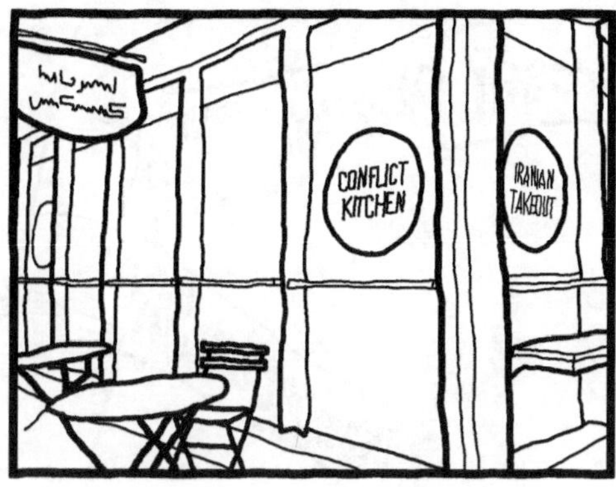

Jon Rubin, Dawn Weleski

Conflict Kitchen

2010-2017

This project consisted of a take-out restaurant in Pittsburgh that served only ethnic foods from countries with which the United States was in conflict. The menu focused on one nation at a time, rotating every 3-5 months, and features related educational programming.

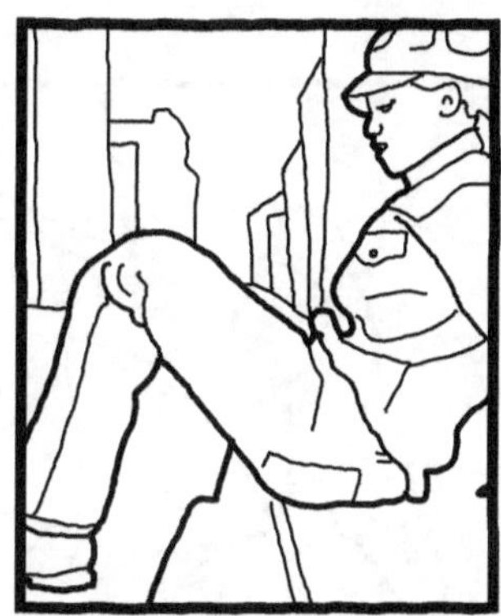

LaToya Ruby Frazier in collaboration with Liz Magic Laser

Performance in Front of Levi's Photo Workshop

2011

Frazier carries out a choreographed series of movements grinding a pair of jeans into the sidewalk in front of a temporary Levi's Photo Workshop in SoHo, protesting Levi's co-opting of the image of Braddock, PA — a town in economic decline — for promotion of jean sales.

https://art21.org/watch/new-york-close-up/latoya-ruby-frazier-takes-on-levis/

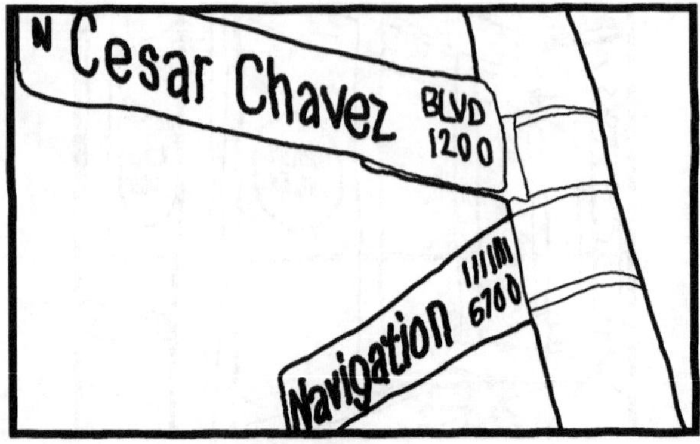

Carrie Marie Schneider

Hear Our Houston

2011–2013

A hub of public generated audio walking tours around Houston, with the goal of hearing 'Houston in your words and to walk a mile in your shoes.'

http://www.hearourhouston.com

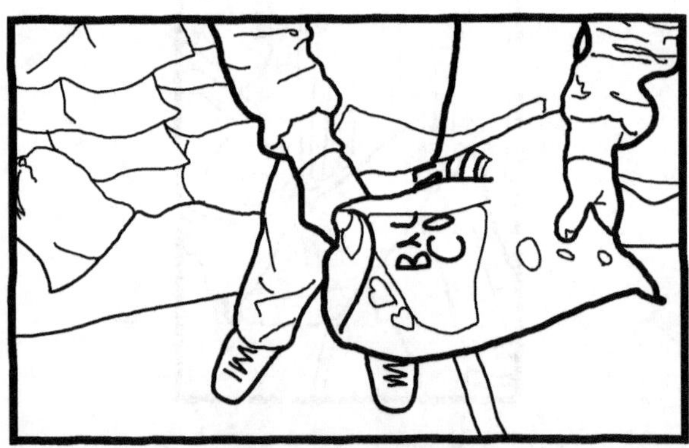

Michael J. Strand

Fargo Sandbag Project

2011–ongoing

Strand has distributed thousands of sandbags to area schools, day care centers, and assisted living centers during the Fargo-Moorhead flood seasons. Participants who were not physically able to assist in sandbagging by showing their encouragement through writing and drawing messages on the sandbags.

http://www.michaeljstrand.com/#!fargo-sandbag-project

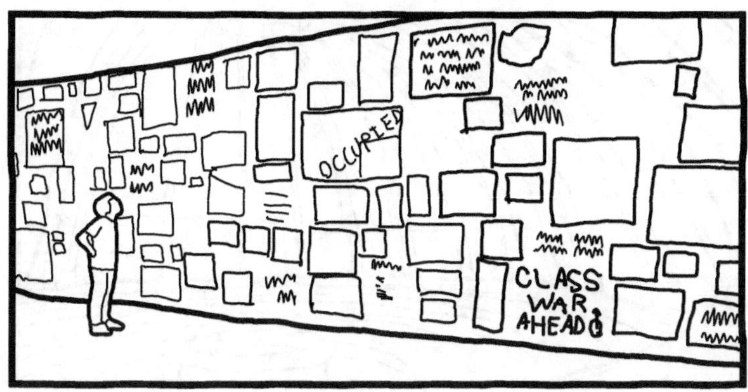

Jason Lazarus

Phase 1 Live Archive

2011–ongoing

This archive of Occupy Wall Street signs recreated from online documentation of worldwide occupations are made collaboratively with the public, and used for ongoing public occupations and display.

http://old.jasonlazarus.com/project_1_187/
phase1livearchive2011present

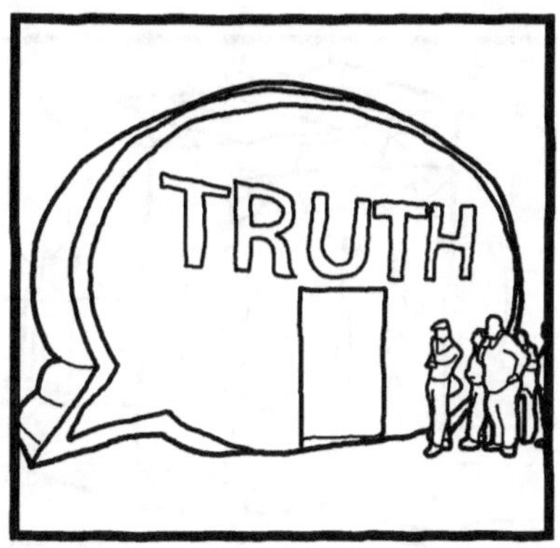

Cause Collective (Hank Willis Thomas, Ryan Alexiev, Jim Ricks, Will Sylvester)

The Truth Booth

2011–ongoing

This is a giant inflatable speech-bubble-shaped video recording booth traveling the world… *In Search of The Truth*. Participants are asked to record two-minute video responses as they finish the statement, "The truth is…."

http://www.causecollective.com/projects/
httpwww-insearchofthetruth-net/

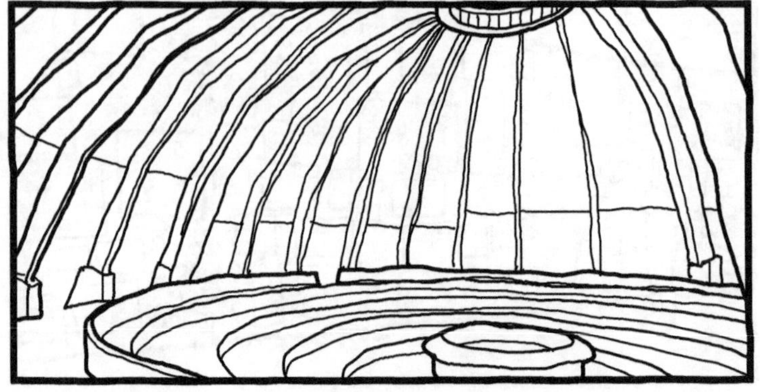

Jonas Staal

The New World Summit
2012-16

This was an artistic and political organization dedicated to providing "alternative parliaments" hosting organizations that found themselves excluded from democracy. There were six of these summits.

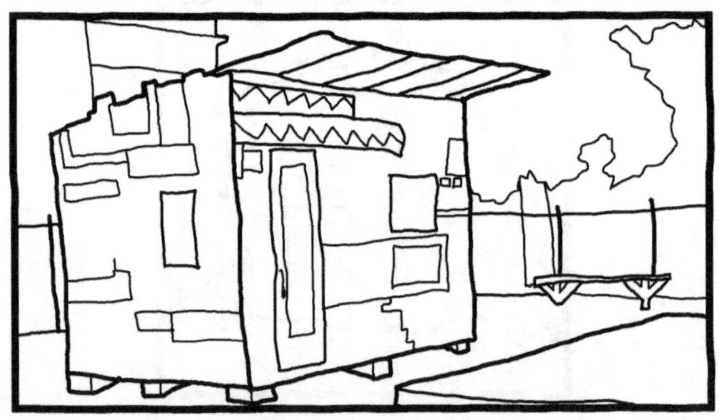

Faheem Majeed

Shacks and Shanties
2012–ongoing

A multifaceted ongoing installation initiative serving as a temporary home and collaborative platform for artist interventions, performances, civically engaged community members, and organizations.

https://shacksandshanties.tumblr.com/about

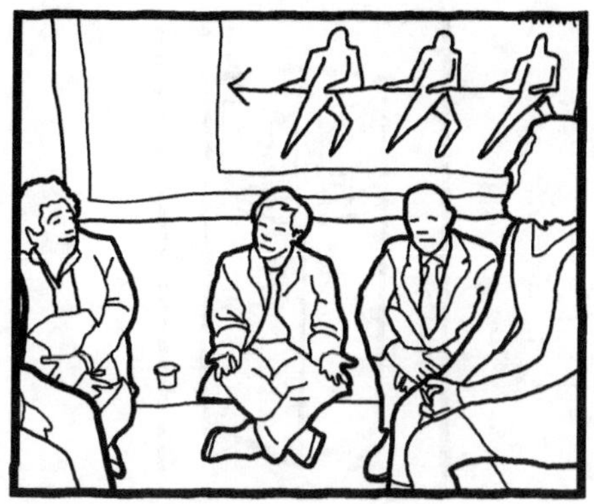

Pedro Reyes

People's United Nations (pUN)

2013

This project takes the form of a conference where 193 regular citizens, who live in the region and are connected by family ties or by birth to the nations represented at the UN, apply techniques and resources from social psychology, theater, art, and conflict resolution to geopolitics.

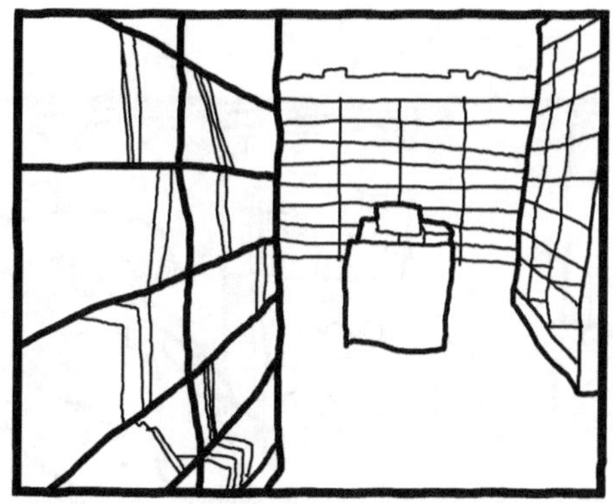

Pablo Helguera

Librería Donceles

2013-ongoing

This project began with establishing the only bookstore of Old Spanish-speaking books in New York because 2 million people speak Spanish in New York City and very few books and bookstores available in Spanish. It has since traveled to multiple cities throughout the US.

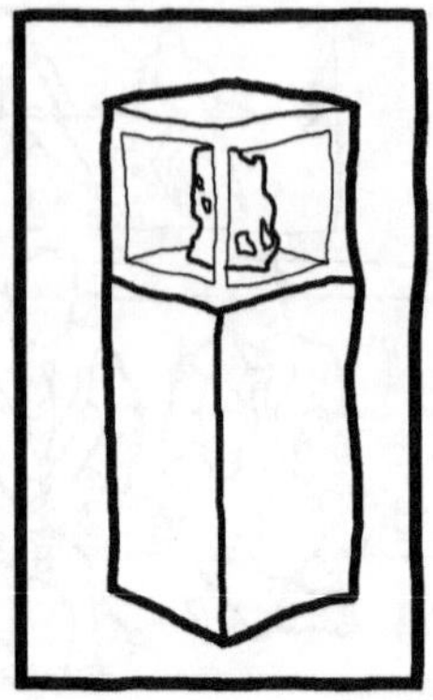

Trevor Paglen

Autonomy Cube

2014

This work is designed to be housed in art museums, galleries, and civic spaces where it creates a Wi-Fi hotspot routed over the Tor network, a global network of thousands of volunteer-run servers, relays, and services designed to help anonymize data. When **Autonomy Cube** is installed, both the sculpture, host institution, and users become part of a privacy-oriented, volunteer run internet infrastructure.

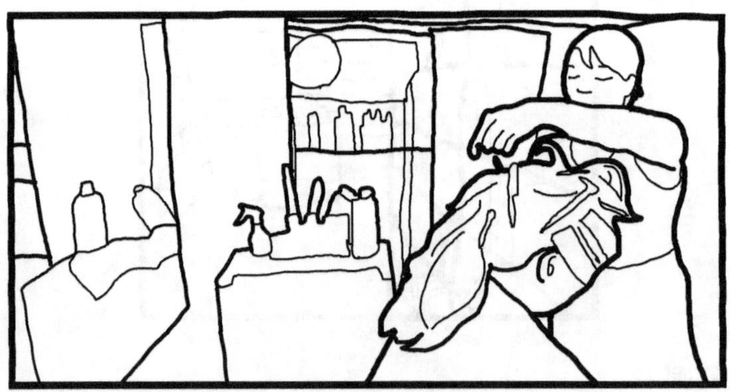

Jody Wood

Beauty in Transition

2014

This work included a mobile, outdoor beauty salon serving the Denver homeless population, and an audio/video installation within the RedLine exhibition space showcasing interviews with participants.

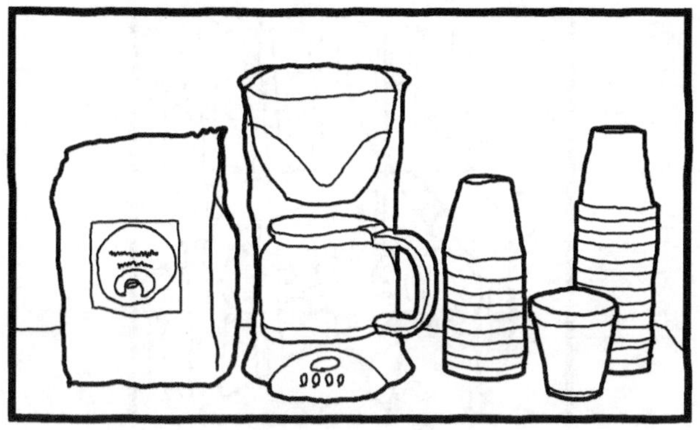

Fran Ilich

Diego de la Vega Coffee Co-op

2014

This project aimed to connect rural agricultural workers in Mexico's Zapatista communities with service industry laborers in New York City by serving Zapatista-grown coffee at catered events throughout the city.

```
http://www.abladeofgrass.org/fellows/
sea-fellow-fran-ilich/
```

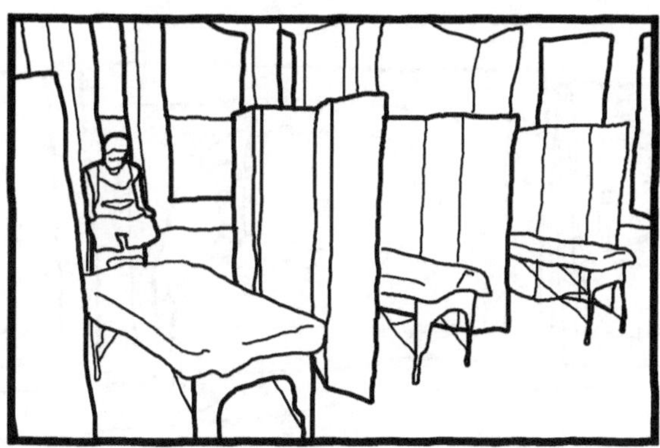

Simone Leigh

Free People's Medical Clinic

2014

Leigh converted the home of the late Dr. Susan Smith McKinney Steward, the first Black woman doctor in N.Y. State, into a temporary space that explored the beauty, dignity and power of Black nurses and doctors, whose work is often hidden from view.

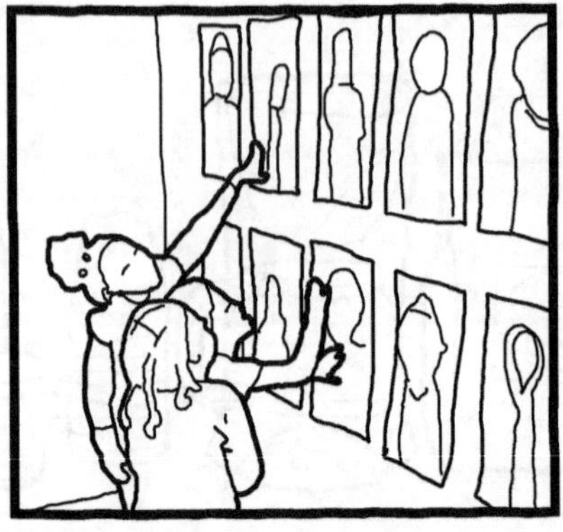

Lisa Jarrett and Harrell Fletcher

KSMoCA, King School Museum of Contemporary Art

2014–ongoing

This contemporary art museum inside of Martin Luther King Jr. School (PreK-5th) in NE Portland, OR, has collaboratively developed programming with the school's community, local university students, and a team of artists.

http://www.ksmoca.com/

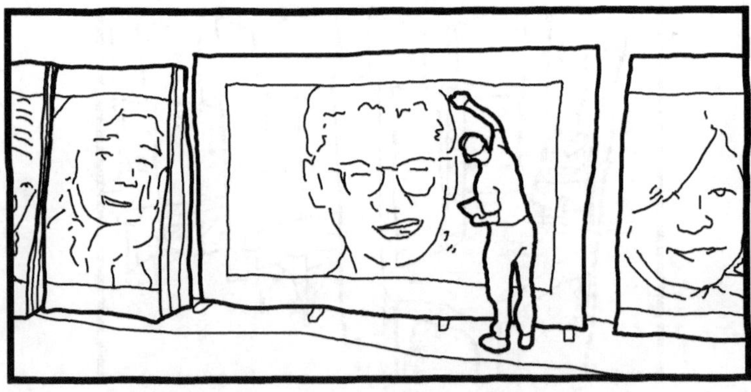

Brett Cook

Reflections of Healing (ROH)

2014

Through participatory public art installations and wellness clinics, this project promoted health equity.

http://www.abladeofgrass.org/fellows/brett-cook/

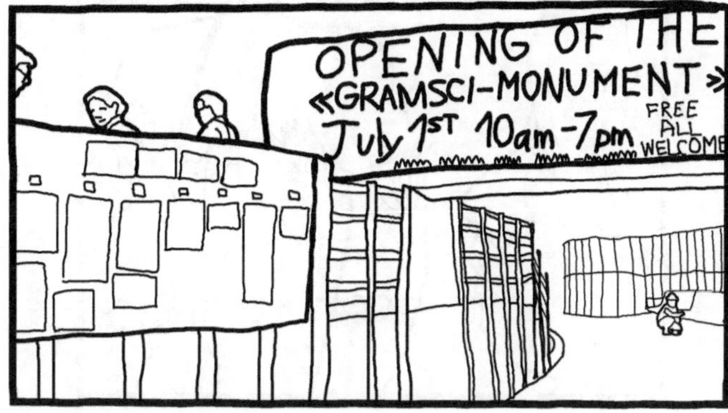

Thomas Hirschhorn

Gramsci Monument

2015

Hirschhorn collaborated with residents of a Bronx public housing development to create a temporary sprawling installation which posed political and philosophical questions about what a monument can be.

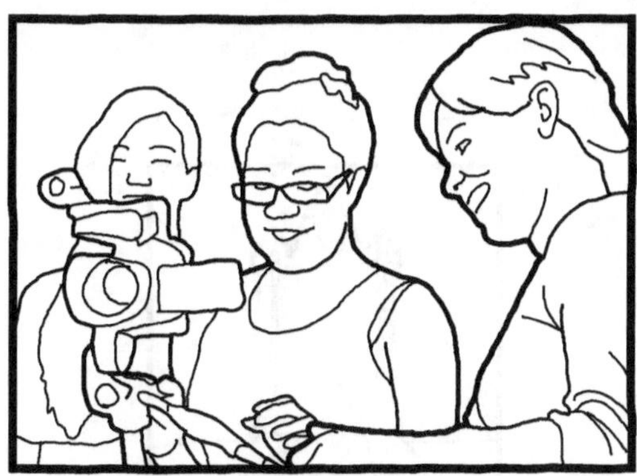

The Center for Urban Pedagogy

Stand Clear of the Rising Fares

2015

CUP worked with Teaching Artist Christina Houle and students from five Bronx high schools to investigate why transit costs what it does and who decides. Students interviewed a number of stakeholders. They created a short documentary video to share what they learned.

http://welcometocup.org/Projects/UrbanInvestigations/
StandClearOfTheRisingFares

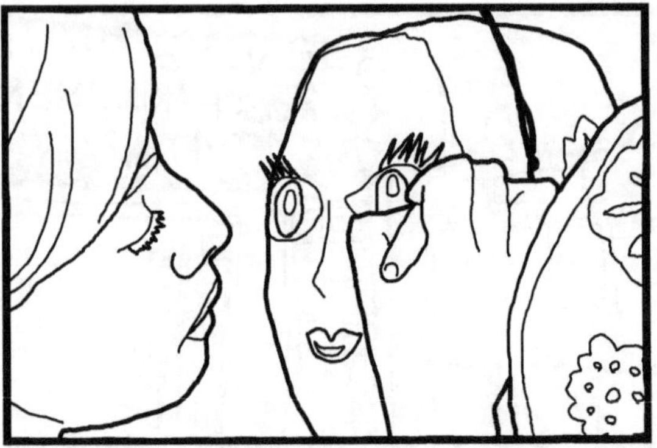

Dignicraft

The Collaborative Piñata

2015

This project explores the lives of 4 Purépecha families who make piñatas that get sold across the border in the United States. The project brings attention to families, who migrated over 1,500 miles over 20 years ago for a chance at a better life near the border.

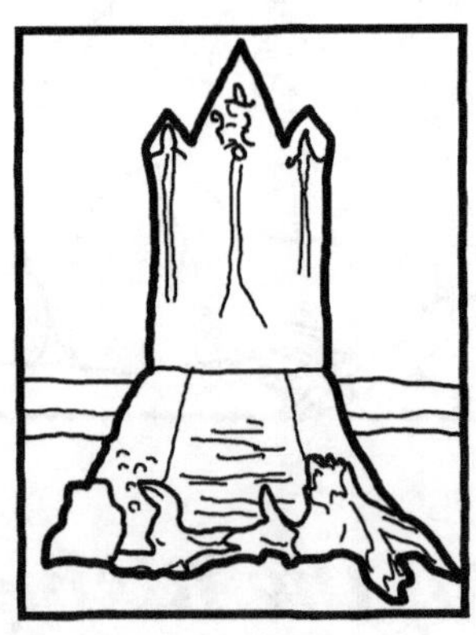

Linda Weintraub

Grandmother Earth

2015

A participatory installation on the wall and floor of the gallery, made from organic matter from local woods. Throughout the exhibition, viewers were invited to expand upon the artwork by contributing their own 1-foot square additions.

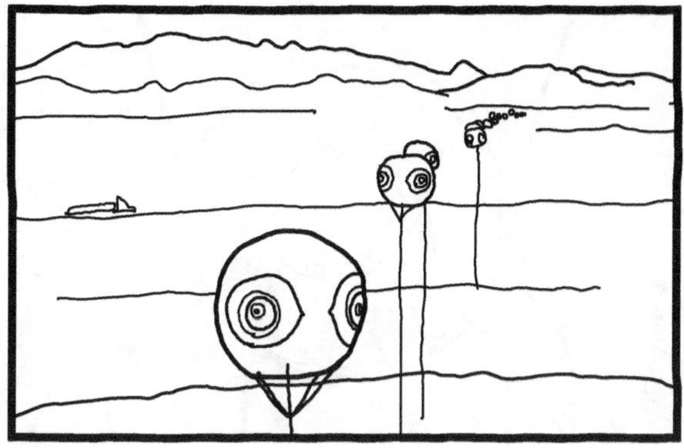

Postcommodity

Repellent Fence

2015

This 2 mile floating fence made of 26 balloons was meant to spark dialogue between indigenous, United States, and Mexican publics and their government agencies to create a more safe, healthy, and culturally appropriate borderlands environment.

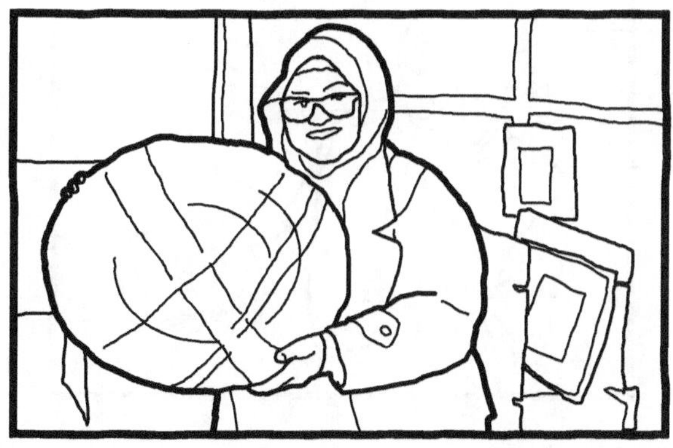

Larsen Husby, Julia Caston, Mac Balentine

Minneapolis Art Lending Library

2015–ongoing

Four times a year, the MALL hosts Lending Events in venues across the Twin Cities, and the public is invited to come browse the collection and take a piece home with them for three months, for free.

http://www.artlending.org/

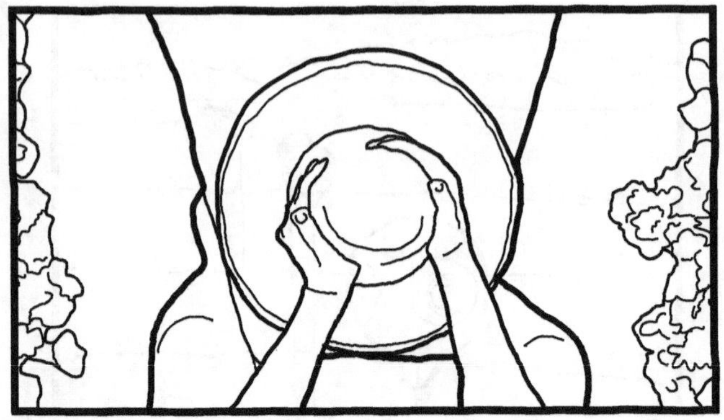

Amanda Leigh Evans

From and To Dust
2016

Long-term collaborative urn project. Each person brings their own perspective on death and mortality, and an openness to engage complex conversations on these topics.

`https://amandaleighevans.com/From-and-To-Dust`

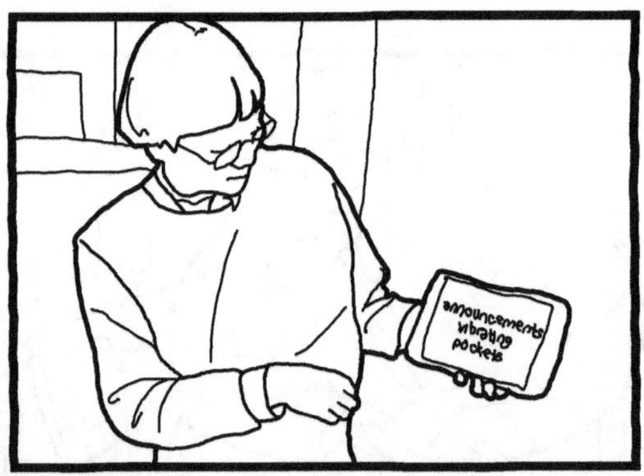

Christine Sun Kim

(LISTEN)
2016

On a sound walk through the Lower East Side, the artist emphasized layers of subjective, interpersonal, and technical mediation involved in non-verbal communication. Attendees were encouraged to re-evaluate how to experience sound in space, and space as sound.

`http://christinesunkim.com/work/240/`

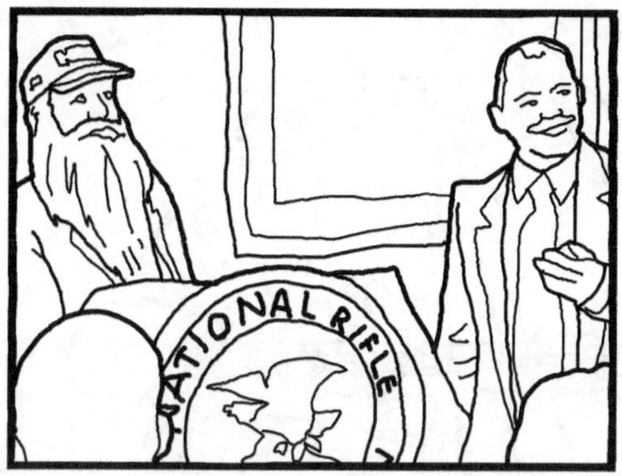

The Yes Men

Share the Safety
2016

In this hoax NRA press conference, The Yes Men announced a fake campaign to "buy one, give one" in order to get guns into the hands of the under-armed economically disadvantaged citizens (homosexuals, the elderly, people of color). The real NRA disavowed the campaign.

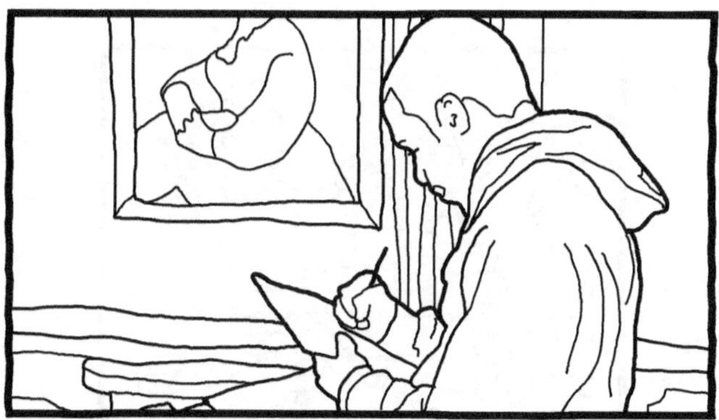

Maia Chao and Josephine Devanbu

Look at Art, Get Paid
2016–ongoing

A socially engaged art project that pays people who don't visit art museums to visit one as guest critics of the art and its institution, thereby reversing the relationship between the educator and the educated, the paying and the paid.

http://www.lookatartgetpaid.org/

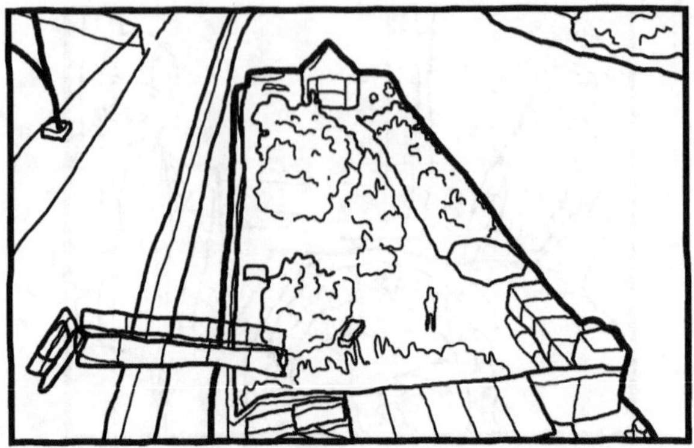

Mary Mattingly

Swale
2016–ongoing

A collaborative floating food forest dedicated to rethinking and challenging New York City's connection to its environment.

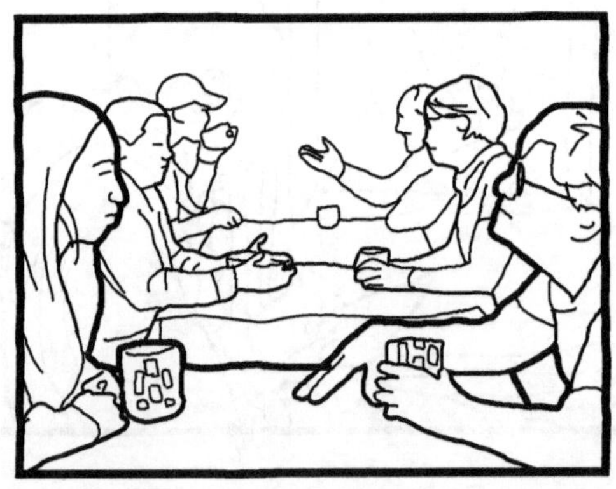

Lauren Karle In collaboration with Jeni Hansen Gard

Weaving Dialogues
2016–ongoing

Tea and conversation guided by prompts left by other participants embroidered on a table cloth allow people to connect people through shared conversation and to experience handmade objects.

http://www.laurenkarle.com/weaving-dialogues

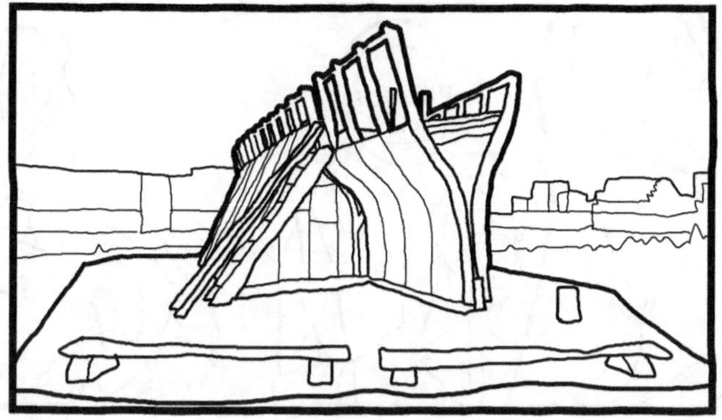

Future Farmers

Flatbread Society Bakehouse

2017

Built with local boat builders, the hull of this "ship" hosts three bread ovens for making a variety of bread types and the main form is insulated with locally-sourced rammed earth.

`http://futurefarmers.com/projects/bakehouse`

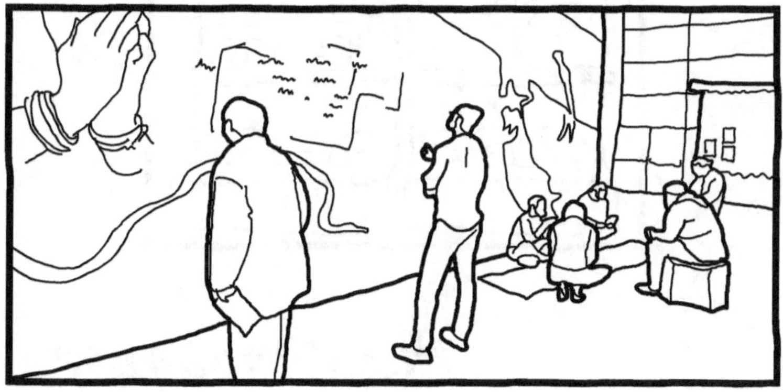

Jeanne van Heeswijk

Philadelphia Assembled

2017

Through programs, meals, and installations throughout Philadelphia, this project brought together hundreds of collaborators to tell a narrative about the city's history and possible futures.

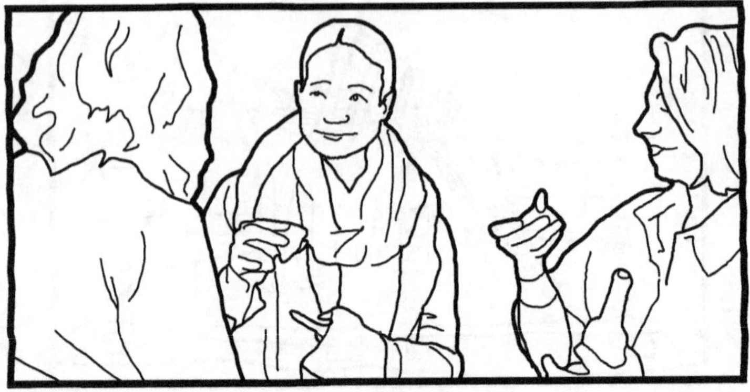

M.C. Baumstark

Menstrual Cup Project

2017–2019

A fun, destigmatizing performance with cocktails and souvenir ceramic menstrual cups to casually approach menstruation and its cultural connotations.

```
http://www.c3initiative.org/social-objects-nceca-
exhibition.html
```

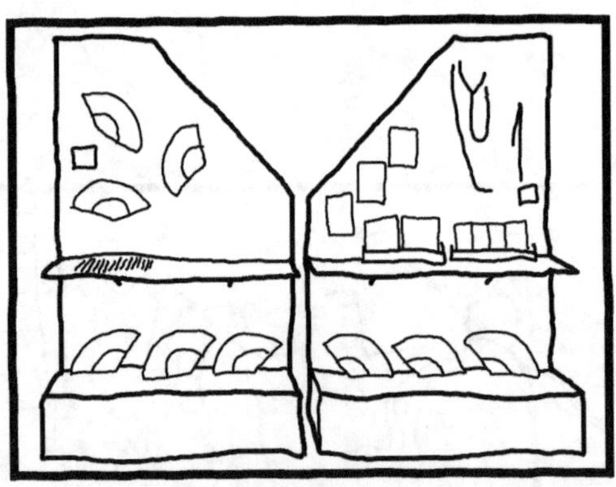

Nancy Nowacek

M__________, the Menopause Project

2018

A pop-up shop created to bring visibility and attention to a topic still shrouded in mystery, shame, and isolation in a storefront space where the public can, learn, reflect, and share experiences of menopause and aging.

```
http://nancynowacek.com/m__________-the-menopause-project
```

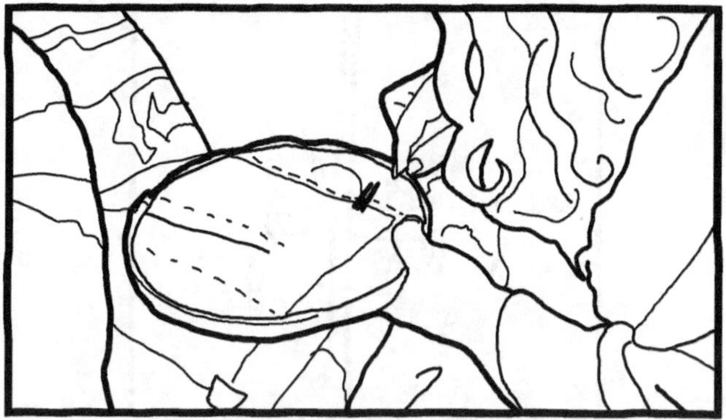

Catherine Reinhart

Collective Mending Sessions
2018–ongoing

For the duration of this project, I will be inviting friends, acquaintances, and strangers to mend alongside me.

http://www.catherinereinhart.com/new-gallery-4/

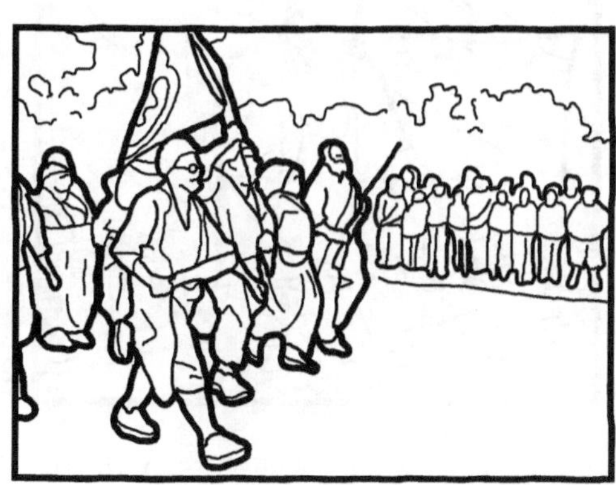

Dread Scott

Slave Rebellion Reenactment
2019

It reimagined the German Coast Uprising of 1811 which took place just outside of New Orleans. The project featured over 200 re-enactors and was documented by John Akomfrah.

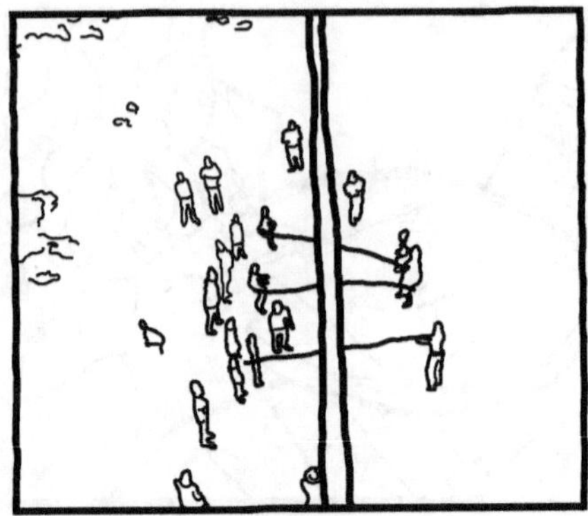

Virginia San Fratello and Ronald Rael

Teeter-Totter Wall

2019

Playful and meaningful seesaws installed on the border fence between the U.S.-Mexico border.

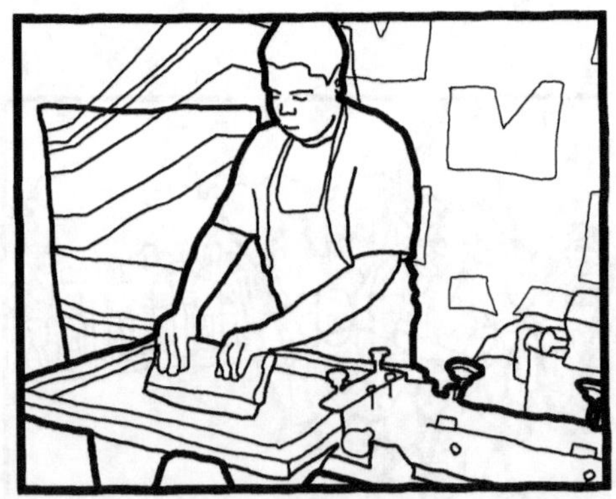

Transformazium (Dana Bishop-Root, Leslie Stem, Ruthie Stringer)

The Neighborhood Printshop

Offers design and printing services, youth out of school time programming, and an open teaching and learning studio. It also creates paid positions for local users through a shop tech training program.

http://transformazium.org/

Appendix

15 WEEK SYLLABUS

WEEK 1 -- Definitions, Spectrums, Intersecting Fields, Craft and Social Practice

> Selected reading from ***Education for Socially Engaged Art***

> Selections from **History 1900-1920s**

WEEK 2 -- Systems / Topics, Discussion Questions

> Selected reading from ***Education for Socially Engaged Art***

> Selections from **History 1930-1950s**

WEEK 3 -- Forms/Approaches, selections from Skills

> Selected reading from ***What We Want is Free***

> Selections from **History 1960-1970s**

WEEK 4 -- Tips for Effective Social Practice (more skills)

> Selected reading from ***Teaching Community: A Pedagogy of Hope***

> Selections from **History 1980-1990s**

WEEK 5 -- Evaluating Projects (more discussion questions)

> Selected reading from ***The Questions We Ask Together***

> Selections from **History 2000-Present**

WEEK 6 - Project 1 – Planning

> Selected reading from *Living as Form*

WEEK 7 - Project 1 – Working

> Selected reading from *Art and Social Practice Workbook*

WEEK 8 - Project 1 – check-in on progress

> Selected reading from *Participation is Risky*

WEEK 9 - Project 1 – Concluding

> Selected reading from *Art Against the Law*

WEEK 10 Project 1 – Reflections

> Selected reading from *Immersive Life Practices*

WEEK 11 Project 2 – Planning

> Selected reading from *Institutions and Imaginaries*

WEEK 12 Project 2 – Working

> Selected reading from *The Practice of Public Art*

WEEK 13 Project 2 – check-in on progress

> Selected reading from *Beautiful Trouble*

WEEK 14 Project 2 – Concluding

> Selected reading from *Artificial Hells*

WEEK 15 Project 2 – Reflections

> Plus reflection on class as a whole

* Remove **PROJECT 2** for a 10-week class.

SAMPLE EXERCISES

REFLECT ON POSITIONS OF PRIVILEGE

Use Jamie Utt's 2012 exercise from *How To Talk About Privilege To Someone Who Doesn't Know What That Is.* [http://everydayfeminism.com] Start with a piece of paper folded in half, and write down the ways in which you are privileged on one side, and the ways in which you are not on the other. Working in pairs or small groups, listen to each other discuss both sides of the paper.

ANALYZING CONNECTIONS WITH OTHERS

In the text, *The Questions We Ask Together* (Open Engagement, 2015), Crystal Baxley outlines an exercise for analyzing connections, thereby heightening our awareness of all our connections. See pages 56-57 for this simple check-box reflection exercise.

PRACTICE HAVING BETTER CONVERSATIONS

Refer to Celeste Headlee's Ted Talk on *10 Ways to Have a Better Conversation*. See if you can embody all 10 recommendations. Try breaking into groups of three, and having one person observe a conversation using these 10 recommendations as a checklist or notes sheet.

PRACTICE THOUGHTFUL RESPONSE IN DEBATE

In Paul T. Corrigan's article, ***Getting Students to Talk to Each Other, Rather Than the Teacher***, [http://teachingandlearninginhighered.org] he calls out five types of comments: affirmations, elaborations, connections, questions, and divergences. Read about calling out each type of comment, which requires self-reflection and constructive participation in dialogue.

PRACTICING FIVE SKILLS FOR SOCIAL PRACTICE

In the text, ***The Questions We Ask Together*** (Open Engagement, 2015), page 376, Renee Piechocki lays out ways to practice five skills identified as useful for social practice: dowsing, endurance, humility, optimism, and storytelling.

GENERATING GROUP PRIORITIES

[http://studycollaboration.com] Ghana Think Tank presents an exercise for generating group priorities on a topic using a matrix for ranking and scoring.

EXAMINING THE LOGIC OF A PROJECT

In the text, ***The Questions We Ask Together*** (Open Engagement, 2015), page 281, Dr. Marnie Badham outlines three suggestions for examining the logic of a project and grounding its relevance in existing theory to prompt answers to a project's "why" and "how."

HONOR A GROUP

In the text, ***Social Objects*** (Socially Engaged Craft Collective, 2017), page 109, Holly Hanessian lays out instructions for celebrating or honoring a group working on behalf of social justice, the environment, or others. This exercise asks students to reflect, plan and execute a gesture of gratitude.

EXERCISE RESOURCES

MULTIPLE EXERCISES IN A SINGLE BOOK / WEBSITE

Baumstark, Mary Callahan, and Amanda Leigh Evans.
*Social Objects: Socially Engaged Craft Theory, Practice
and Action*. Socially Engaged Craft Collective, 2017.

Boal, Augusto. *Games for Actors and Non-Actors*.
Routledge, 2010.

Boyd, Andrew, and Dave Oswald Mitchell. *Beautiful
Trouble: a Toolbox for Revolution*. OR Books, 2016.

Charpentier, Erin, and Travis Neel. *Art & Social Practice
Workbook*. Publication Studio, 2013.

Sholette, Gregory, and Bass Chloë. *Art as Social Action:
an Introduction to the Principles and Practices of
Teaching Social Practice Art*. Allworth Press, an Imprint
of Skyhorse Publishing, Inc., 2018.

Woolard, Caroline, and Stamatina Gregory. *STUDY
COLLABORATION*. 2016, studycollaboration.com/